ABOUT THE BOOK

"**SHE IS THE GIRL** I should have married." Jaap Polak remembers thinking this when he first saw Ina Soep in 1943 at a party in Amsterdam, Holland. For her part, Ina Soep saw Jaap Polak accompanied by his wife of four years, and thought to herself, "They do not belong together, they are not suited to each other at all." This first meeting marked the beginning of a poignant love story lasting more than fifty-five years.

It was 1940 when the Nazis overran Holland and occupied it. Deportation began a few years later for all Dutch Jews, and Jaap and Ina met up again in the transit camp of Westerbork, Holland, when Jaap negotiated an arrangement for him and his wife to be assigned to Ina's barrack there. Jaap pursued Ina in earnest from then on, never wavering in his passionate love for her, yet remaining ever loyal to his wife for the benefit of their mutual survival, in spite of their unhappy marriage. When his wife strenuously objected to Jaap's attentions to Ina, enduring camp gossip about her "husband's girl friend," Jaap and Ina began writing letters to each other which continued until after their liberation in 1945.

The actual LETTERS are the origin of this book, collected and saved until now in their original state. The story combines their intimate correspondence with the vivid images of daily concentration camp life as it was actually experienced and recorded by them, then and there. Augmenting their LETTERS, written on any scraps of paper available, are descriptions and related accounts that reveal powerful examples of their optimism, their faith in the future, and the unshakable love that sustained them through all the daily horrors that were visited upon them both, and the unbearable conditions during the later months of incarceration. After liberation, Jaap's divorce, and Ina's and Jaap's marriage, they emigrated to the United States in 1951 with two young sons, settling in Eastchester, New York, where a daughter was born to complete the family.

steal
a pencil
for me

Love Letters from Camp
Bergen-Belsen
Westerbork

JAAP POLAK   INA SOEP

LION BOOKS PUBLISHER SCARSDALE

2000

THIS IS A LION BOOK

PUBLISHED BY LION BOOKS

Copyright © 2000 by Jaap Polak and Ina Soep Polak

All rights reserved under International and Pan American
Copyright Conventions. Published in the United States
by Lion Books, Scarsdale, New York.

Lion Books and the Lion Colophon are registered trademarks of Lion Books.

Library of Congress Cataloging-in-Publication Data
Polak, Jaap, 1912-
    Steal a pencil for me: love letters from Camp Bergen-Belsen and Westerbork / Jaap
Polak & Ina Soep.
    p. cm.
    ISBN 0-87460-395-1
    1. Polak, Jaap, 1912- - -Correspondence. 2. Soep, Ina, 1923- - -Correspondence. 3.
Jews- -Netherlands- -Amsterdam- - Correspondence. 4. Holocaust, Jewish
(1939-1945)- - Personal narratives. 5. Westerbork (Concentration camp) 6. Bergen-Belsen
(Concentration camp) 7. Netherlands- -Biography. 8. Germany- -Biography. I. Soep, Ina,
1923- II. Title.

DS135. N6A157 2000
940.53'18'0922492—dc21
{B}
                                                                                    00-057631

Paperback Edition
ISBN 87460-374-9
First Printing   August 2002

Manufactured in the United States of America

DEDICATION

This book is dedicated to the memory of Jaap's parents:
FREDERIK POLAK
and
GRIETJE ASSCHER-POLAK

Jaap's Sister:
JULIA POLAK-BOLLE

Jaap's Brother-in-Law:
PHILIP DE LEEUW

Ina's Brother:
BENNO SOEP

Ina's Best Friend from 1935 until his Deportation in 1942:
RUDI ACOHEN

And all our Relatives and Friends who Perished in the Holocaust

We also dedicate it to our Children and Grandchildren, in the hope that they may continue to live in a world where such a disaster will never be permitted to occur again.

Ina and Jaap Polak

ACKNOWLEDGMENTS

This book would never have come into existence if it had not been for the early accomplishments of our daughter, Margrit Betty Polak Shield in translating our letters from the Dutch, and editing notes dictated by us. Margrit wishes to convey special thanks to her friend, Scott Klavan, for his help with the completion of her last draft. The collection was presented to us as a gift at our fortieth wedding anniversary celebration as a precursor to a book.

We wish to thank our friend, Dr. Harriett L. Chandler, now the State Representative of the 13th Worcester District in the State Legislature of Massachusetts, who, for many years, consistently urged us to have the letters translated for publication; and our friend and colleague, Lawrence Goldstein, for conducting such a fruitful search for the right publisher.

And to Harriet Ross, our Editor, we extend our appreciation for her thoughtful, probing, and insightful queries and suggestions during our many meetings, which enabled us both to revisit the experiences we endured during those years of misery and upheaval. With her valuable assistance, the collection of letters and notes has indeed been developed to become the book we hoped for.

Ina and Jaap Polak
September 2000

CONTENTS

EDITOR'S NOTES

The experiences of Jaap Polak and Ina Soep give life and breadth to the long-gone voices that speak to us through the horror known as the Holocaust; because their story is unique in its testimonial to the unbelievable resilience of the human spirit in withstanding increasing blows of physical suffering and heinous indignities. The love that developed between them during their internment years was love in its purest form; and its strength sustained them through the miseries of disease, starvation and despair, keeping alive their determination to survive. This enduring bond was heightened by the LETTERS themselves–written then and there with no conception of how their lives would eventually evolve.

The original letters were written on all sorts of paper: whatever was immediately available to the writers-torn, dirty scraps, sometimes a regular white sheet of typing paper, even toilet tissue. Some were almost illegible, others well preserved.

About Ina's letters, she had this to say: "On the day I was liberated by the men of the American 9th Army, I was about to be lifted into one of the Army trucks by a soldier when the bottom of my rucksack fell out, spilling all my meager belongings on the ground. The threads of the stitching had totally rotted away after more than one and a half years of being stored in very damp places, under bunk beds in the barracks. Someone thrust an old battered suitcase at me, and I quickly stuffed all my things into it–except the letters. There had been a very heavy rainfall, and the ground was a mass of large, muddy puddles. The letters which I had kept at the very bottom had fallen into one of them. I still have a vivid image of myself staring down at them and having to decide very quickly what to do about them. At that moment, the most important sensation was of being free, and the letters seemed of little significance then. I left them there.

How could I have known that fifty years later they would be of interest to others, and I might like to share them? However, while I may have forgotten the exact words I used then, I have not, nor will I ever forget my feelings or my thoughts when I wrote them."

Therefore, in response to Jaap's letters, Ina paraphrases herself and does share her recollections of that time frame wherever relevant.

The chapters on the Early Years of both Ina Soep and Jaap Polak have been added to the collection of Letters to broaden the context and background in which their stories unfold. Excerpts have been drawn freely from the oral histories, recorded in their interviews for the Survivors of the Shoah Project of the Visual History Foundation, and from their own additional, anecdotal remembrances of life in the concentration camps which follow the Letters. In doing so, we have attempted to retain a conversational tone to the entire manuscript, believing that the best way to expand our understanding of the years leading up to deportation, and afterward, in the camps themselves, is to allow the survivors to tell their own experiences directly to the reader.

Harriet Ross

——■ ■——

The icons inserted between the LETTERS and recollections are used as symbols of separation and confinement of the principals, Ina Soep and Jaap Polak.

THE FIRST MEETING

Ina Soep. (pronounced "Eena Soup")

In Holland, birthdays are always a big celebration, so you are always attending a birthday party of someone you know, be it relative, friend, or acquaintance. I had heard from my girlfriend about a very nice couple she knew who would be at a party we were going to in June 1943. When I was introduced to them, the first thought that went through my mind was that this "nice couple" did not belong together at all. They just simply did not seem suited for each other. I forgot about them the minute after I made that observation.

Jaap Polak: (pronounced "Yahp Pollack")

When I was introduced to Ina at the party, my first thought was, "Now, this is the woman I should have married." Even though my wife, Manja, was a striking and charismatic woman, and we had loads of friends, our marriage was not a happy one. She presented many problems to me with her quickly changing moods and her open flirtations; and Manja felt she married too young. So we considered separating after the war. However, we promised Manja's mother to stay together and support each other throughout the war. Indeed, Manja was protected by my "special" papers; therefore, it was imperative to remain bound as a couple.

HOLLAND IN HISTORICAL CONTEXT

Jews have been in The Netherlands since the early fourteenth century, when groups arrived there after having been expelled from France and England.

In 1536, Spanish and Portuguese Jewish refugees from the Inquisition were permitted to settle there; and Dutch cities, especially Amsterdam, became centers of Sephardic Jewry. Throughout most of its history, Holland has been a haven for Jews fleeing oppression in other countries, and thus it attracted Askenazic Jews as well.

Civil registrations of births, deaths, and marriages began in Holland with Napoleon's conquest of The Netherlands in 1811, and continued after his defeat. These records have been kept in The Netherlands for close to 200 years; and the most significant information contained in this national repository of data also includes religious backgrounds, mixed marriages, conversions, etc. In this manner, it became a simple task for the Germans, upon conquering the Dutch, to methodically and immediately identify all Jews in Holland in all Civil Registry Offices in the country.

Holland, by virtue of its geographical position and its topography, was particularly vulnerable to invasion by the Germans. It was virtually a "sitting duck", surrounded by the open sea to the North

1

and West, bordered on the South by occupied Belgium, and on the East by Germany itself.

Added to that, the terrain of Holland is flat, bereft of mountains and woods or other natural hiding places. The dikes, which in the past, had always been a valuable military deterrent to most invaders, were deemed useless and of no consequence in thwarting a military strike by the Germans.

As late as 1940, notwithstanding the downfall of Czechoslovakia, Poland, and Norway to Hitler's advancing forces, the Dutch still believed Holland was impregnable, wrapped in the secure cloak of protective neutrality, relying heavily on their water barriers to deter attack. They were, tragically, wrong. Indeed, despite solemn and repeated promises to the contrary, Hitler literally violated the Dutch neutrality, once it had become clear that England and France were prepared to fight on after the fall of Poland.

On May 10, 1940, German planes and land forces crossed the Dutch frontier as paratroopers dropped at strategically important points behind Holland's defenses. The first bombings flattened the city of Rotterdam on the fourth day, May 13. The Dutch recoiled under the first large-scale airborne attack in the history of modern warfare. One day later, under threat of inflicting the same fate on Amsterdam and the rest of the country, Holland capitulated, giving Hitler a victory with lightning rapidity. Unable to arrest the impending disaster for her nation, Queen Wilhelmina departed with her cabinet to live in exile in England.

All of this factored into creating a steel trap for the easy capture and control of all the Dutch Jews. It doomed 140,000 of them who lived in all of Holland, 100,000 of whom lived in the city of Amsterdam alone. For the next five years, the five days of savage German attacks would henceforth darken this civilized country. It marked the beginning of the end of Dutch Jewry.

THE EARLY YEARS
JAAP POLAK

I have always said that I have had three lives. My first life started when I was born on December 31, 1912, 87 years ago. My second life began with the German invasion in Holland in May 1940, and ended on April 23, 1945, when I was liberated by the Russian Army. That day I succumbed to spotted typhus, went into a coma, came out of the coma on April 25, and for me, that was the day my third life started.

My first, early life was wonderful: peaceful, happy years spent with my Orthodox Jewish parents and three sisters. I can trace my family back three hundred years in Holland; and we had always enjoyed complete freedom of religion. Every Jewish New Year, I went to blow the Shofar in a girls' orphanage, and once in a Dutch prison for the Jewish inmates. Although we had a very restricted Orthodox upbringing, it was accomplished in a beautiful way. We had very little else in our lives to take the place of the closeness of large, frequent family gatherings, and the sociability of communal religion. Every Thursday night, fifteen or twenty family members would get together in someone's house; and every summer we went to the seashore or some other resort place; but the only way we could afford this was to take in paying guests. We were poor and struggling, but I never really felt poor.

My father was an accountant who not only supported his own family, but also provided for his three sisters and their families. My mother worked as a teacher of shorthand and embroidery in a Jewish Day School. She was an Asscher–she came from the extended family of one of the two most prominent diamond manufacturers in Holland, the Asschers. The other was the Soep family.

As for my education, it consisted of attendance at an elementary Orthodox Day School, and a commercial high school. It was then I decided I needed some experience with non-Jews. After graduation, I worked for three years at the Carlton Hotel in Amsterdam as a secretary. That was very important to my entire life–and I still try to make up for all the wonderful food I missed eating there because of my kosher restriction! I would have loved to have remained in the hotel business, (it teaches you so much about life); but I left to study a specialized division of accounting: tax consulting. After graduating, I became a certified tax consultant and joined my father's practice. He was the accountant, and I was the tax specialist. It was a great pleasure to work with my father in our firm.

Our family embraced Zionism; in fact, my father was a founder of the Mizrachi movement, the Orthodox branch of Zionism. I still treasure a photograph of my father shown with Chaim Weizmann and Vladimir Jabotinsky in Amsterdam in 1921. My years in the youth movement of the Mizrachi were wonderful years, being a part of a group of dedicated young idealists, many of whom left for Palestine in the Thirties. The goal was to create a permanent Jewish state.

I met my first wife, Manja, in a Zionist summer camp. We were married in 1939. I was 26, she was 20. We were both very outgoing and had many friends, but it was not a good marriage. Both of us agreed to a separation; but when the war started, we decided to stay together until it ended.

Very few Jews left Holland, as we had the mistaken belief that in case of another war, Holland would stay out of it as it did during World War I. But when the Germans invaded Holland, we all felt that it could be the beginning of a horrible time. However, none of us thought that our lives would be in danger, and that mass killings were in the offing. Then, the departure of Queen Wilhelmina, who had been the personification of religious freedom, came as a tremendous blow to us.

For me, the years of the German occupation of Holland until my arrest were worse than any subsequent experience I had in any concentration camp because of the incredible tension and insecurity—not knowing what terrible thing would happen to you next. As soon as you were made to be different wearing a Jewish Star on all your clothing, you were looked upon as a Jew, not as a Dutchman anymore.

In July 1942, the Germans started raids all over Amsterdam, because Jews were not reporting for deportation when they received their notices. If the Germans had a call for 2,000 Jews, only 200 would appear. So they wanted to show us that those who appeared when they were called would go to labor camps, while those who disobeyed would go to concentration camps. That wasn't true, but that's how they threatened us.

On July 14, 1942, Bastille Day, I was doing my work as an accountant for one of my clients in the Jewish Quarter; and while I was working, the SS sealed off that area, sealed my office, and took me, along with 400 other Jews, and marched us through Amsterdam. At one point, they took me and nine others and put us against a wall. Ten SS men came forward with their guns drawn, and I remember saying the Shema, the prayer that a Jew says when his end is coming. They shot into the air, and marched us along again. We got to the square where the SS headquarters were located, in the Euterpestraat, and they put all the women in the center; and the men had to run and run around the women. The SS came and took pictures of us, laughing their heads off. We saw members of the Jewish Council coming and going, trying to negotiate what they were going to do with us. That night, we slept in the corridors of that building, on the floor; and the next day we had to walk and sometimes run around the women again. Later that afternoon, they asked us about our professions; and I remember not knowing what would be a good profession to mention, and what would be a bad profession. All I know is that when I said "accountant", I got a kick in the pants and was allowed to leave. I remember running around the corner to an old lady who was a client of my father's and then going home, not being able to believe what had happened. I think that almost having been killed, and then being set free, gave me a tremendous willpower to live; and I thought that nothing worse could ever happen to me, although that also turned out not to be true.

After that I felt that I could survive anything, even the terrible waiting for a knock on the door in the middle of the night to be taken for deportation. I think I avoided immediate deportation for me and my wife by working as an accountant in the apparel industry which was forced to manufacture uniforms for the German troops. We all wanted to believe we would be going to labor camps to work; we knew nothing of the different camps and imminent danger we faced. Everyone tried to save himself by any means possible...at first by having a useful job because the skill of the Jewish workers was sorely needed. But you believed that if you were "good", and obeyed all the decrees carefully, you would go to a labor camp. At one point, I was granted a very particular privilege by a "good German" whom I happened to know. I could ride on a street car with a special pass, but I was not permitted to sit down. You also knew that if you did not obey these laws, or if you were poor and unimportant, you would most likely be shipped to a concentration camp where you would be mistreated and perhaps die there.

The two years of the German Decrees slowly pauperized us. We gradually lost all our possessions, our property, our businesses, and our freedom. It culminated on April 29, 1942, when all Jews in Holland were forced to wear the Jewish Star. Earlier, in February 1941, the Jewish Council had been established to function as a liaison agency between the occupying Germans and the Dutch Jewry: a direct line of communications. The Jewish leaders were men of prestige and importance in the community. But when, on July 1942, the deportations started, they were obliged to provide the Germans with lists of Jews to be taken for deportation each week. They never realized that they were making life and death decisions as they had no knowledge of the existence of extermination camps.

The options to avoid deportation were varied. People had to secure so-called "protections." One of the "protections" was to be on the "Palestine List" which my father and mother were privileged to be on, since my father was a prominent Zionist. But when the certificate in their names arrived, they had already been deported from Westerbork to Sobibor. So I prevailed upon the Jewish Agency which handled the process to have the names of my parents changed to mine, my wife's, and my younger sister's. And when this was granted to us, we were "privileged" to be sent to the concentration camp, Bergen-Belsen, from where the exchange ultimately took place on July 1944, but only for 200 people. No money was ever paid for this.

Another "protection" was to be on the "Weinreb List." I had paid $50.00 in Amsterdam for three people; me, my wife, and her mother, to be on that list. Weinreb was a Dutch Jew of Polish descent who convinced the Germans in Holland that he had connections with some of the high authorities in Germany. They had supposedly told him, "You can give us a list and we will protect those people." It was a list of people who would be destined for Madagascar. We were issued a stamp for that. It was all later proven to be fictitious, but the Germans believed him. Everybody wanted to be on that list, of course, and paid varying amounts of money to be placed on it.

7

Then there was the "120,000 Stamp." If you paid 120,000 guilders worth of diamonds per person, that would protect you too with its special number. This would be roughly the equivalent of $50,000 per person.

In spite of all the "protections," and there were many, many more, deportations progressed at a very rapid pace, and we were eventually caught up in them. In July, 1943, my wife and I were arrested in a raid that brought us to Westerbork, the transit camp, where I was reunited with my parents who had been sent there two weeks earlier.

I grew up in a totally mixed neighborhood in Amsterdam. As Jews, we were very much a minority. There was a Jewish Quarter, but that was mostly inhabited by the poor, working people. It was called Jodenbuurt, where Rembrandt had once lived and painted.

I would say that we were an affluent family, except that I didn't quite realize it as a child, because in those days money was never talked about. My parents wanted their children to believe that we should live modestly. We were often admonished, "Don't spend too much, –don't smear your butter so thick on your bread; it went up a penny last week." We could have fruit, but only one piece for dessert, never two. We could have only one candy a day before we went to bed. It was all very strict and confined to rules.

My father was a leading diamond manufacturer. He owned a factory where the entire procedure of transforming diamonds from the rough stone to finished gem was executed. His was the second largest factory in Holland. My mother was like all the mothers in those days. She was a housewife, and she took care of the family. Of course, there weren't very many appliances in the house, so it was a big enterprise. We had a large house and two maids, and mother was still always "doing." When we were little, we always had German nannies who taught us German, including children's songs and poems. Then too, my mother, was of German descent.

As a family, we were observant Orthodox Jews. In Holland, you were not a member of one synagogue. You belonged to the Jewish community in your town or city. Actually, in Amsterdam, there

9

were two separate groups, the Ashkenazic Jews and the Portuguese Jews. You paid taxes according to your income, a certain percentage of it–like you did to the city that you lived in.

Amsterdam had about 100,000 Jews. For many years, my father was president of the Dutch Jewish Head Synagogue which was the governing body of Amsterdam Jewry. This was Ashkenazi only. My father, as Chairman, plus a large administrative staff ran the Jewish community of the city. All the synagogues in Amsterdam belonged to this entity.

In the Thirties, I never noticed any anti-Semitism, personally, although I'm sure there was some. The old Dutch nobility with all the titles still existed. There were some clubs that you couldn't join. There was a rowing club, one big businessmen's social club; there was a tennis club where you could not go if you were Jewish, but there was never any overt anti-Semitism that I experienced. People, in their hearts, may have felt they didn't want to socialize with Jews, but nothing was ever said. It wasn't even written about. I mean, as a child, you didn't know what it was. Many of my friends were not Jewish.

In the late Thirties, when the German Jews came to Holland from Germany, there was more of an anti-German feeling even among the Jews. We saw them more as Germans than as fellow Jews, but we did feel obliged to support them as a refugee group.

In 1937, my family moved to a new, beautiful house. In those days, most people didn't own their houses, but you considered it your own home anyway.

Life was very peaceful; but in retrospect, we all had blindfolds on. In the summer of 1939, when I was sixteen, I visited England to learn to speak English fluently. I stayed with a German Jewish family in London because they were kosher. In the middle of

August, my father called me back from England and said, "It looks like war in Europe." He thought Holland would be safe. Holland was going to stay neutral again and not be involved in a war, if there was one. That's how we reasoned that nothing was going to happen.

However, some Dutch families left for America. They thought it was not a good idea to stay in Europe, and we considered them almost traitors. How could they leave Holland?–such a wonderful country that had always been so good to us.

Then on May 10, 1940, we woke up at about 4 o'clock in the morning and heard the droning of airplanes, and shooting and bombing; and we knew we were being invaded by the Germans. I think that some authorities were warned that it was going to happen, but they wouldn't believe it, and it never leaked out to the population. It was called "The Invasion." We had always felt very safe also, because there was the so-called "water line" that they thought the Germans couldn't cross over. We would just flood the middle of Holland, and the Germans would never get their troops through, never thinking they could just fly over and drop their troops which is, of course, exactly what they did.

During the five days of the attack, we had to go into hiding in cellars and basements whenever the alarms went off and we thought we would be bombed.

On May 14, 1940, many Jewish people committed suicide, especially those who were in the Socialist movement whose names were known to the Germans; and many Jews who didn't believe they could survive a German occupation after knowing what had happened to the Jews in Germany. Late that day, after Rotterdam was bombed mercilessly, and Amsterdam was threatened with the same fate, Holland surrendered.

11

The Germans now occupied The Netherlands. They proclaimed that they would do nothing to harm us. They would abide by Dutch laws, and we could keep on living the way we always had. Nothing would happen. I don't know if we really believed them or not, but we wanted to believe them.

At first we lived more or less normally as we had done before. There was no distinction as yet between Jew and non-Jew. I went for an entire year to a school where I was being trained to become an executive secretary. Among many subjects, I learned shorthand, and typing, and business correspondence, all in four languages.

Nothing happened to us until my brother was caught and arrested by the Germans during a reprisal raid. A German soldier had been killed in his neighborhood. My father began pressing the authorities for the release of my brother, trying to use his influence as an appointed member of the prestigious Jewish Council, the liaison between the Germans and the Jews in all occupied territories. All information, regulations-everything was conveyed through the Jewish Council. They almost succeeded in freeing my brother, when unexpectedly, on June 22, 1941, Germany broke its pact with Russia and invaded it. Now the many Communists in Holland became the enemy. They were immediately arrested and placed in the Dutch military camp vacated by all the young Jews, including my brother, who were all quickly deported that same day to Mauthausen, the most notoriously cruel Austrian camp known for its rock quarries. Those unfortunates sent to this camp were forced by threat of death to climb 148 stone steps carrying huge blocks of stone, and were not permitted to use the steps in descending, but were forced to slide down on the sides of the steps where loose pebbles created unsure footing, resulting in serious injuries to many prisoners. A few months later, we received a death certificate. They informed my parents that my brother was "auf der Flucht erschossen," ("shot while trying to flee"). My mother always said, "as if they would give you a chance to run!" After the war, we learned that he, like many others, had been stoned to death on the long steps leading to the quarry where he had to work. Our family was devastated.......

In late 1941, the German Decrees began to be issued. Every week, the Jewish Weekly newspaper of Amsterdam was ordered to publish the new Decrees on its front page. It was all done very gradually, very orderly, and officially.

First, every Jew had to buy and wear Jewish stars. You had to cut long strips of stars into individual ones, and then sew them on all your clothing. If you didn't wear them and the Germans discovered you were Jewish, you were arrested. Our credo was always, "The war won't be that long, and as long as we can stay here, no matter what they tell us to do, we will have to do it." We had to turn in our radios, our silver, and our jewelry. We had to hand in our bicycles, and we couldn't use the streetcars. We, of course, had no cars anymore. We could only shop after 4 o'clock in the afternoon in an outdoor market. We weren't allowed to go to the stores any longer. With every new measure we always said, "Well, it isn't so terrible as long as we are home and can remain in our own house, in our own country." Then, in July 1942, mass deportations began in earnest.

In May 1943, the Germans followed and arrested a woman who had come to our house to bring us fresh produce. Unbeknown to us, she was Jewish and an active participant in the Resistance movement. The Germans wanted to arrest us too, but my father used his influence with the President of the Jewish Council for his contact with the highest SS Commandant in Amsterdam. He ordered the arresting 'Green Police' to release us. However, the Germans had seen and liked our house, and wanted to occupy it.

Two days later, they returned and we were told to quickly pack our things. We were sent to the Jewish Theater in Amsterdam. Our house was kept intact for German usage-one of only two Jewish homes in the city that were not emptied.

Usually, when people were arrested and deported, the Germans would seal the house. The very next day, a moving van would pull up in front of the house. There was one moving company the Germans used by the name of PULS, and from that, a verb was created. The house was "pulsed" that day after people were taken; and the furniture was sent to Germany for victims of the Allied bombings.

As one of the Decrees previously given by the Germans, the Jewish Theater we were sent to, (formally called the City Theater), had been the only one where Jews could attend. They could only produce performances by Jewish writers and composers, presented by Jewish actors and musicians. Now, it was transformed into a detention hall where they brought people who were caught in raids or were arrested before being sent to the camp in Westerbork. We were detained in the Theater for five weeks, much longer than most transients. Others were sent out with the next train. Fortunately, we were released, again through my father's influence in the Jewish Council, with the condition that we would not return to our own home. Then the Germans forced us to rent an apartment in the last Jewish ghetto where we lived for ten weeks.

On Rosh Hashanah, September 30, 1943, the dreaded knock on the door signaled the rounding up of all remaining Jews in our area of Amsterdam.

As had been ordered by German Decree, our rucksacks were always packed. So we were quickly ready and prepared to leave.

WESTERBORK
DEPORTATION CAMP

Westerbork was originally set up before the war by the Dutch government as a camp for German-Jewish refugees who came to Holland without money, or Dutch connections with relatives, or friends to sponsor them. The establishment of the camp angered the German Jews, making them feel unwelcome by confining them to the dreary Northeast of Holland. When the Nazis invaded Holland, barbed wire was placed around Westerbork; and the Nazis designated this camp as the eventual deportation center for all Jews in The Netherlands. From there, they would be sent off to concentration camps in the East. The long term German-Jewish residents became the administrators, setting up a Jewish hierarchy, and ruling with an iron hand. German Jews were given preferential treatment over the Dutch Jews, and some of their leaders even dressed and acted in the manner of SS men.

The German Jews were in charge, but there were also German guards in the watch towers. There was a German Commander, who lived in a nearby villa. He told the German-Jewish hierarchy in the camp what he wanted done; and they executed what he demanded.

When Jaap Polak and his wife, Manja, arrived in Westerbork in July of 1943, approximately 75,000 of Holland's 140,000 Jews had already passed through and had been sent off to either Auschwitz or Sobibor, the notorious extermination camps. Eventually, 103,000 Jews were deported from Westerbork of whom only 3,000 returned to Holland after liberation. Of the remaining numbers, 24,000 went into hiding or joined the Resistance movement. Of this group, 16,000 survived. About 1,700 escaped to other countries; most of them returned after the war.

ARRIVAL IN WESTERBORK
JAAP POLAK

The September 1943 transport was the last transport with two thousand people in it, which was the final clearing out of the Jews from Amsterdam. The Germans completed this action on the day of the Jewish New Year, September 30, 1943. All of the most prominent Jews were on it, because they were the ones who had been able to hold out the longest. The two Presidents of the Jewish Council, Abraham Asscher, Holland's foremost diamond merchant, and Professor David Cohen, the Classics specialist, had finally arrived, although many of the sixteen members of that Council had already been deported. The Soep family had also enjoyed added protection because of their diamond business. When I learned that the Soep family came, I remembered the beautiful young woman I had seen a few months before at the birthday party, and I knew I wanted to see her again.

When our barrack was closed, we were dispersed; and since I knew someone in the Housing Department at the camp, I arranged to have my wife and me transferred to her barrack. That was how I was able to re-introduce myself to her. When I approached her at

17

first, she was polite but skeptical, especially when she asked me about my wife. But when I explained that my marriage was a bad mistake for both of us, and that we later intended to get a divorce, she seemed to believe me. I wanted so much for her to believe me! Call it intuition, but I knew she was right for me the moment I laid eyes on her at that birthday party; and the more and better I got to know her on our walks and talks around the camp, the more I was convinced it was a heaven-sent union meant for a lifetime. I had no doubts; and I was determined to dispel her doubts. I wanted to protect her and care for her–and love her. For me, her welfare became a daily concern. As it grew more and more difficult to see each other, we began to exchange little notes and letters.

ARRIVAL IN WESTERBORK

INA SOEP

We were arrested in Amsterdam and taken by train to Westerbork. Then we had to walk for a mile from the train to the camp. When we finally arrived in the middle of the night, we first filed into a huge Registry Hall. From there, we were all sent to the barracks. I vividly remember the barrack we were quartered in; Barrack 64. It was pitch dark, everyone there was asleep when they turned on the lights; and we were assigned to some of the empty bunks that were stacked in three tiers for about one hundred people.

The camp was located in totally inhospitable surroundings. It was on a heath; very, very dry, sandy, and windy, with many storms occurring, and very sparsely populated because of the kind of unforgiving land it was. Westerbork itself was nondescript. It was built on one long, narrow stretch of earth with fields in back of it, and on each side were the barracks. Besides those, there were other barracks where the camp work was done. The entire atmosphere was utterly cheerless and bleak. The barracks were even more dismal, with the sand seeping through every crevice. The ground turned to mud with every downpour. It was ugly and filthy.

19

We were there for a few weeks, when the man I had briefly met (of the "nice couple" at the birthday party I attended with my friend a few months before in Amsterdam), moved into our barrack with his wife, Manja. After he approached me to make sure that I remembered who he was, he slowly started to show me more and more attention. I never had the feeling that he was being merely flirtatious; in fact, it was obvious that he was totally smitten with me, and vigorously started to court me. I hedged a lot. I hardly knew him; he was so much older and more experienced than I, (a settled man, thirty years old; versus me, barely an adult at twenty). Moreover, as I reminded him regularly, I still counted very much on the return of my boyfriend, Rudi, whom I had known since I was twelve and he thirteen, until his arrest and immediate deportation after a German reprisal raid in his street. Jaap confided his sadness and disappointment in his marriage, and how he and his wife were only remaining together to have a better chance of staying alive.

They had promised Manja's mother to stay together and support each other until the war was over. He explained how they considered separating before the invasion. His confession about a mutually desired separation was definitely offered in response to one of my first reactions after I realized he was pursuing me. "But you are married. What about your wife?" Nevertheless, I was convinced, in spite of myself, of his obvious sincerity and honesty in answering my queries, and dispelling any lingering doubts I harbored about the depths of his feelings for me which he quickly proclaimed to be very serious. We started taking walks together at night between dinner and curfew. We walked between the barracks, within the perimeter of the camp where the barbed wire ran, where we could walk for a half hour or so. It was very dark in the evenings, as there was no outdoor lighting except for flashlights. Everyone called the center path through the camp the *Boulevard de Misères* where most people walked, so we avoided that. But there was always a time limit for us to be alone, since there was a nine o'clock curfew. Nevertheless, we became good friends, and built up a solid base of compatibility and trust. That's how our courtship started.

However, we could not forget that Jaap's wife was there in the camp too. The barrack was divided into two sides with the entrance in the middle. On the right side were the men; on the left side were the women. During the day, we could intermingle. We could have our meals together. There were tables between the beds with benches, and we could sit there; but at night, of course, after curfew, we couldn't. His wife and I could practically see each other. She usually didn't mind about us; but sometimes she did mind a great deal. It was a troublesome source of embarrassment for her, because everyone could see me and her husband together so much. Sometimes, she would be very nice to him or to me; and other times, she would forbid us to see each other. That was why we started to write notes to each other which continued all through that time in Westerbork.

"By the barracks chased her,
Where I first embraced her;
Over there.
This is my Westerbork love affair."

*–part of an original Dutch song,
"Westerbork Serenade," written and
performed by the popular Dutch
duo, Johnny and Jones, for one of
the Westerbork cabaret revues.*

LETTERS

Westerbork, Tuesday, November 16, 1943

My always dearest girl,

I want to write and let you know how much, in the very short period of time that I have known you, I love you. Actually, although I shouldn't say it, the last few months have truly shown us that what we feel inside cannot be held in, no matter how difficult the situation, either circumstantially or socially.

I feel when I'm with you, and crazily enough, when I'm not with you, a sense of peace that I have never really known with any other girl. I have the feeling that we completely understand each other, even when we don't speak a word; and if this is true, then things are going to be so very good between us.

I had aspired to a perfect marriage in my first marriage, but knew from the first day that it would never happen. With you it will be different and better; but we must thoroughly discuss how we will live our lives, as I am convinced that in working together, we can build an ideal life. Here, however, it is so difficult, considering all the problems we shall eventually face, problems we don't even know about yet.

I do want to write more to you, but I have already told you how very difficult it is to put my feelings into words, much less write them!–especially, because of the last few years of my marriage with Manja, when I had to work it all out from inside myself. With you, it can be different. That I feel now, because I feel more of a similarity in character with you in a few weeks than in the seven years that I have known Manja.

Let us agree to tell each other everything, including the day to day things which are often so important. And, later, if we are to have a normal, day to day life together, it is especially important for us to be completely honest with each other as that is the only way to build up a good relationship.

Now sweet darling, it is as if I am preaching like an older to a younger person, but that is not the case. It is my good fortune that when I am with you, I do not feel older than you; and perhaps the difference in age is something that we will suffer from only in theory, and not in practice.

Sweet Ineke, I wanted to courier this letter to you yesterday, but I had to write in between work in five installments. And these five installments form a whole, indicating that you have not been out of my thoughts for one moment. That makes me very happy. I hope you feel the same way.

Many kisses,

Jaap

> *Ina*:
> In spite of myself, I was drawn to this interesting man who was so persistent in his affections for me. He began to paint a future for us; and while respecting my constant references to my boyfriend, he, nevertheless, must have instinctively felt that life was so tentative and subject to change under our terrible circumstances, that he had a good chance of being the man of my life. I was intrigued, and probably flattered, by his strong attraction to me—it was a much more mature approach to love than I had ever experienced. At first, we shared our hopes and dreams for ourselves with each other, then gradually included one another in those dreams.

———■ ■———

Friday, November 19, 1943

My dear, dear Ineke,

I have nothing to do, and when I have <u>nothing</u> to do, I have only <u>one</u> thing to do, and that is to think of you. We have some days in store in which we will speak less to each other than usual, and as unpleasant as this is, I do believe that our mutual feelings will grow even when we speak less to each other. When you are with me, I always have the feeling that we understand each other completely, thus comes the complete peace which governs our relationship.

Considering the circumstances, we have had it quite good here, but no doubt there will be some days, or perhaps even spells coming, in which everything will be more difficult: Manja will give us a hard time, and we won't be able to take walks, perhaps having little or no chance for close contact. You must not let this discourage you. Even if unavoidable things happen, which I'd rather not think about, but which we must consider in our calculations, we must find strength in the knowledge that there is someone here who makes life worth living, and with whom it might soon be possible to build a new life.

If I look and see in how many ways our characters are alike, then I really believe that there is little chance that a marriage between us could fail. Know above all, that, in my mind, I hold a vision of an ideal marriage in which man and wife share a mutual goal, and in which each complements and supports the other. We must often go and hear good music; we must go and see good theatre, and in exactly this way grow closer to each other.

I think a lot about this: That if there is anything wrong in our relationship, it is that you are afraid of the fact, that due to my unfortunate marriage with Manja, I was driven into the arms of the very first girl I saw as available. I hope and believe that this is not how you see it; because I do consider the marital period, and perhaps even more importantly, the premarital period, too important to abuse for pleasure's sake. On the other hand, the seriousness with which

26

I began this relationship brings consequences for both you and me that could create difficulties in the future. For me there is only one possibility, and that is to "conquer" the girl I love, if that is still necessary, without losing sight of future difficulties. These will be ultimately harder for you than for me... I only hope that the choice will not be too difficult for you.

I must stop as I have to get back to the school to work. Sleep well; think that you are lying in my arms, and then I am sure that you will find you rest nicely.

Good night, sweet girl of mine. Till tomorrow.

Many, many kisses,

Jaap

———■   ■———

Jaap:

When I first arrived at Westerbork in July 1943, I worked digging canals outside the camp, which I hated.

We all tried to get important jobs to do-to make ourselves indispensable to the Germans. Fortunately, some professors came to the camp who knew me, and I was asked to help them out in setting up classes. Luckily for me, I had worked with children in the Mizrachi Zionist organization, so I was made principal of the school in the camp, after working my way up from teaching to administration; and then, when the previous principal was deported, I was assigned to take his place.

We had to have a school, because someone had to look after the children while the parents worked. We tried to make life bearable for the children from kindergarten age through high school with books sent from Amsterdam, and teachers to teach them. Unfortunately, it was a school that admitted, five hundred children one Tuesday, and deported the same five hundred the following Tuesday. It was really traumatic to have them for one week, or sometimes a few months, and then see them disappear.

It was a difficult job, emotionally as well as administratively, because there were children and professors constantly coming in and going out. And there were university professors who had to teach second grade level because I had no other classes for them. Sometimes I taught; but the important thing was that the children were taken care of while in Westerbork.

My job also included arranging classical musical concerts at the school. It was important that we had a cultural environment, to keep up your morale; so you didn't feel completely dead.

The Germans attended these events too. In the camp, there were many of the best musicians from the Concertgebouw Orchestra and other famous groups of artists. The musicians thought that if they performed they would have a better chance of remaining in Westerbork; so they did their very best, singing, dancing, playing their instruments. There were also cabaret evenings, in which I was not involved. The Germans loved them.

They would sit in the first rows; and they would assign ten beautiful girls to serve them refreshments. They even allowed them to take off their Jewish stars, but then ordered that they put them back on afterwards.

Ina:

As macabre as it may seem, Westerbork maintained a full-fledged cabaret program which offered six different revues between the summer of 1943 through the following year. They were performed in a large, multi-purpose hall where incoming and outgoing transports were registered, and where German festivities were celebrated by the camp officials. One moment the space would be decorated with SS flags and swastikas, and the next moment with décor for the revues. The stage was built of wood which came from the interior of the synagogue in Assen, the nearest city to Westerbork. There had been a fire of unknown origin inside the synagogue in 1940.

The cabaret revues were performed by the most prominent German-Jewish and Dutch-Jewish theater artists, all residents of the camp. The Commandant even invited high-ranking SS officers from around the country to be entertained by them. He was proud of the performers who were given certain privileges, like the dubious one of being allowed to address the Commandant personally. He also permitted them to fetch costumes and material for props and scenery from Amsterdam. A great deal of care was lavished on the designs and their execution.

The cabaret was immensely popular. After performances, many of the camp inmates could be heard humming the songs. It seemed to give them the strength to maintain a certain optimism, notwithstanding the misery and uncertainty surrounding them.

Still the cabaret was certainly not appreciated by all. Many Jews were appalled that fellow inmates performed for the Germans amidst such tragic circumstances. They refused to attend any of the shows. A cabaret with top artists in a concentration camp. It is one of the most significant examples of the biting contrasts which occurred within the barbed wire enclosure at Westerbork; where it was possible that in one single day, on a Tuesday, innocent victims would be transported in cattle cars to a certain death; while in the evening, at exactly eight o'clock, Jewish entertainers, singers, and musicians executed a first rate revue.

Participation in the cabaret was a reason for not being transported for the time being. One performed to stay alive-even if family members were deported that same day. But then, in Camp Order No. 86, August 3, 1944, the Commandant canceled the entire operation, and all its members were deported.

A similar fate was in store for all the other artists who performed in the classical musical concerts and operettas, all for the personal pleasure of the Commandant, who always sat in the first row in a large easy chair, next to his SS cronies. He laughed a great deal, but never applauded.

———■　■———

Tuesday afternoon, November 23, 1943

My always sweetest darling,

Just a few words in great haste, but I feel the need, as I have spoken to you so little in the last few days. You don't know how glad I am that everything finally worked out that we can still see each other. If that hadn't happened, the time that we would have had would have been too short. I am only afraid that you think that, due to present circumstances, in which I'm spending more time with Manja than before, I will eventually go back to my old "bad ways." I think this even more because one of your girlfriends made a remark in this regard; that you were only around to bring Manja and me back together again. Just don't be afraid of this, please! Because I want to call you my wife; and I hope that Manja and I can eventually become good friends; nothing more. This statement is necessary, first of all for the outside world, which we must of course take into account; and the second wish I have is that I can at least call Manja a good friend in the future. But again, dear darling, don't think because of this that I want to return to my old life.

What more can I tell you, sweetheart? Only that I hope that we will soon have a quiet hour to spend together. This evening? Bye, dearest girl of mine.

Many, many kisses from—

your Jaap

Jaap:

There were several reasons for me to renew my relationship with Manja. The thing that brought us back together time and time again was the fact that our chance of survival was dependent on being together and being on the same "list." If one of us should quit, we would both be deported. It was a matter of survival . Also, our families were very close Her father died when she was very young and in many ways, I felt responsible for her, despite the sorry state of our relationship.

Thursday, November 25, 1943

My sweet girl,

Very quickly, in between my numerous work activities, a few lines; first of all because I know you feel the need for it, and secondly, because now, when you are so miserable, I would so love to be with you, and I can only be with you in my thoughts. I really feel a bit guilty that we went for a walk last night, when you really weren't better yet, but on the other hand, we both had a great time, and that is most important here.

Before I go farther, an apology. Do you think it awful that this letter is typewritten? I hope not. On the one hand, it is far from nice to deal with a love letter written on a machine. On the other hand, whenever I write by hand to you, my thoughts spring from one thing to another, and this seems the best way to communicate for me. It is also a privilege for me to be able to use it.

My darling, this is truly not a special letter, but it is so busy here, I have lost all concentration. You will have to make do with this for today.

Sleep well. Many many goodnight kisses.

Your Jaap.

Friday night, November 26, 1943

My dear darling,

I am lying in bed in an utterly miserable position, (you have to realize that I am lying in the middle bunk); but I just wanted to write a few more words to you. Why? Only to tell you that an evening without you is imperfect for me. Though I regret every hour that you are not with me, it may be beneficial that when we are not together we miss each other, and thus really understand how good everything is between us.

Don't worry about the problems that your sister-in-law has painted for you in all too glaring colors. There is truth in what she said, but I don't think that we will have that much trouble. What I mean to say is that I love you too much. (Not too much in a bad way).

Now my little love, after this short Friday night chat, I'm going to sleep with my thoughts focused on you.

Till tomorrow,

In my thoughts many, many kisses,

your Jaap

Ina:

The "problems" that Jaap referred to were warnings and admonitions that it seemed that everyone was giving to me: "He's too old, his married, he's poor. He's not from the same background."You're too young to be going with this old guy."

We couldn't be seen together as there were many there who knew us. We always met "on the sly."

There were some people in our age group who knew about us, and I knew there was a good deal of gossip in our barrack .Everyone was constantly trying to discourage me.

Tuesday, November 30,1943 8:OO A..M

My dearest darling,

Here we are, you sick in bed, me in the office, and the worst part is that Manja also had to stay in bed, and as always, watching you with those *Argus eyes.* This morning, I asked your father how you are and he told me that you have a light bronchitis. You don't know, or maybe you do know, how much I want to be with you and how much I want to pamper you. But I can, for the moment only write to you that as of early this morning, my thoughts have been with you. So, if due to Manja's sickness, you don't see me as much don't think I'm forgetting you , but I don't need to tell you all this.

You must try to stay quietly in bed , let everyone spoil you, and you will see that in a few days you are completely well again. But don't try to go out walking around too soon. And Our Good Lord is with us in that respect, as the roads are so muddy here that walking is completely impossible.

In the meantime, it is an insane asylum here in the office, which of course makes concentration very difficult.

Just now (9:30) I was in Barrack 64, where Manja was asleep, and so I thought it would be great to visit you. But you were asleep too, which on the one hand was a pity; but on the other hand, it was nice because you probably needed it. Sleep well, darling.

Try and get better fast. In my thoughts I am with you.
Many kisses,
Jaap

The expression Argus eyes, is a common one in Dutch usage, and refers to a person who is vigilantly observant and watchful. It derives from the story of Argus, a Greek mythological being with many eyes, both in his head and body, some of which were always open, who was known to be a zealous watchman. When he was slain by Hermes, some of his eyes were transferred to the tail of the peacock.

Ina:

Manja's bed was quite close to mine. If I lifted my head I could see her. I would talk with her sometimes when she wasn't too mad at me. I think she actually liked me. I always had the feeling that she would have struck up a real friendship with me if Jaap was not between us.

Jaap:

Everyone knew Mr. Soep. He was a respected figure in the Jewish community. He didn't know anything about Ina and me, but I would always greet him when I saw him. In spite of all the indignities suffered by the Jewish men of position as Ina's father, he always managed to maintain an aura of authority and dignity.

———■ ■———

Friday, December 3, 1943

My sweet darling,

It is 4:30 p.m.; my "bosses" have gone to pray for their souls' salvation, and I make use of the opportunity to talk with you. It is really very bad luck that all our chances are taken away. The Argus eyes are everywhere, and so we have to make do with our written contact.

This afternoon when I realized that I had completely forgotten to go to the linen room for the hand towels, I got there at 3:30 p.m., only to find the door locked! It seems that you are indispensable there. I will take a chance and go back tomorrow. The typewriter is needed, so I will handwrite the remaining few lines, and fill the paper with my almost illegible handwriting.

Manja was no better this afternoon, thus I see the continuation of this annoying situation. So, in any case, you should try to get better; but don't hurry up too fast. This afternoon, in between other things, I enjoyed listening to Beethoven's Kreutzer Sonata played by Dr. Weiss, (piano), and Polak, (violin). So very beautiful... My thoughts were, as always–but especially when I hear music–with you. At the moment it is utter chaos here. We have been permitted to teach in the barracks when we can find a space, so we have to make teaching schedules, etc.. I am extremely busy with that, and if I didn't have to teach tonight, then I would have to work anyway.

Eat the peppermints with relish, and also think that I have the same amount as you and am consuming them at the same time.

Darling, I hope that you feel somewhat better.

Go to sleep early tonight. In thoughts I am with you.

Love and sweet kisses,

your Jaap

Ina:

Jaap could not see me in the linen room because I was sick again and not working. I was employed in the linen room at that time, a very desirable job.

The head of the linen room was a middle-aged German woman, one of the original inhabitants of the camp, who was a distant relative of my mother's; and through her, I was able to get this very favored job in the clean linen room. Because of my asthma, my father didn't want me working anyplace where it was dirty; and so he helped get me work there, where I had to learn to patch sheets on a sewing machine very neatly. I did a really good job; but all of a sudden, I couldn't keep that job anymore. It was too soft, too "cushy," and they decided that I should work in one of the hospital compounds which had its own administrators independent from the rest of the camp. I again ended up in the linen room, doing the same thing, folding sheets and towels, and patching where needed. I managed to get Jaap fresh linens, and my family too. The linens were only meant for hospital use. The linens in the camp itself were only for the original German internees who lived in the tiny row houses instead of the barracks. We used the sheets we carried in our rucksacks.

———■　■———

Monday, December 17, 1943

My little darling,

Just a few words because I feel the need for it.

I understand your feelings completely, but you mustn't let them sweep you into a depression. First of all, everything is much better than you think. That is always my motto. Secondly, we must always try to get over depressed moods, however well-founded they may be, as only in this manner can we survive the difficult life here, and rise above them. And if we now see each other somewhat less, we should be strengthened by the fact that our thoughts are completely with each other.

One thing I hope, is that you don't think that I lack guts in these things. I hope you agree with me that it is much smarter to dodge between all the difficulties, than take the risk of destroying everything. Again, don't think of this as cowardice. If necessary, I will do whatever has to be done, but as long as this leads to our wished for results, it wouldn't make sense to act differently.

Now little lady, I hope you feel better, and that you think as many good things about me as I do about you.

Many, many kisses,

Jaap

Ina:

Jaap buoyed my spirits with his indomitable self-confidence. Sometimes I think I "let off steam" just so I could have him reassure me as he always did. I drew strength from his strength. I knew that he would always have the sensible answer for my impatience, and my occasional feelings of hopelessness regarding our strained relationship with Manja, and our daily lives that were fraught with fears.

Saturday, December 25, 1943

My darling girl,

That you "all at once" felt so down tonight is a very natural phenomenon, and really something that I had expected even sooner.

As difficult as it may sound, you <u>must</u> be strong in this as you have been till now. If you get moods every now and then in which everything looks bleak, it is logical, but it will pass. Maybe you can adapt a piece of my philosophy in life: That in everything, even in the gloomiest things, you must look for the sunny side; and even if you can't find any sunshine, you must look into the future in which ultimately, for both of us, <u>with</u> both of us, happiness lies.

The most predominant thing in all this is something that I have already told you: You must trust me one hundred percent! If you do that, your thoughts will be strengthened in many ways.

So we must go on. It is true that many things will happen, and we have to share our thoughts.

The solution that you suggested tonight is not a solution as long as our feelings for each other are as they now stand. I also do know that your doubts were just doubts of the moment, and you yourself know very well that for what we both want, it is the exact <u>opposite</u> of a solution.

Sweet darling, we shall talk it over some more later.

I am now going to sleep and my thoughts are with you; and I really hope that at this moment you are not worrying, but that you lie peacefully asleep.

Many, many kisses,
your Jaap

Ina:

Sometimes I became very weary of having to always consider Manja's role in my relationship with Jaap. Despite Jaap's assurances, I remember often being annoyed and frustrated by the constant manipulation of our emotions by Manja's edicts; so I became very defiant, and suggested in no uncertain terms that we cease with our courtship. Or else, at the very least, I thought Jaap should ignore Manja and her shifting demands.

Even as I said this, I knew inwardly that Jaap would be the level-headed, sensible one to refute this. He placated me in the gentlest, warmest way.

———■　■———

Monday, January 3, 1944

My very dear little darling,

I really should leave out the word "little" on your birthday, as someone who is as "old" as you should not be addressed as such. But nevertheless, I think I will keep calling you that until your 100th birthday! (How old will I be by then?) I am writing this little epistle on my bed; my handwriting is therefore almost more illegible than usual.

You are starting a new year just as I started a new year a few days ago. What it will bring us we still do not know. But if you look into the future with as much confidence, hope, and optimism as I do, I am convinced that the New Year will bring for us the happiness that we both yearn for.

Don't look at obstacles as if they are all black. I continue to feel very badly that the circumstances for us, more specifically for you, are different than in the beginning of our being together here in Westerbork; but here, too, I believe that God is with us. The foundation has been laid, the rest we will catch up with in Amsterdam: and as long as we keep our daily contact, I am satisfied–not satisfied in the sense that I think it is sufficient–but you do understand what I mean. My darling, my very best wishes on this very special day, as turning twenty-one is something special. Let's hope to be able to celebrate both our birthdays next year in different circumstances, and together.

Many, many kisses, and an extra birthday kiss.

Jaap

Jaap:

I had celebrated my thirty-first birthday a few days before, on December 31, 1943. At that time, my friend, Han Maykels, and I drank a whole bottle of cognac that I had smuggled into the camp the previous July. We drank away our sorrows, not knowing if we would survive long enough to celebrate another birthday. It was a drinking of desperation.

——■ ■——

Friday morning, January 7, 1944

My darling Ineke,

For a second time, things are really lousy here in Westerbork because both you and Manja are in bed. This time I'm really only worrying about you because I heard from your papa that you still had *103°* this morning. Moreover, Manja will be allowed out of bed this afternoon, so the situation is only going to be difficult for one day. It is best that I don't come and see you, because tonight I am going to visit our "Kitchen Connection." You will be curious, no doubt, but you must keep your curiosity under control until you are, hopefully, soon recovered.

So sweet Ineke, we have talked. Keep your spirits up, and get better soon. Really darling, we don't have it so bad, and later on we will have it so much better. (Eternal optimist, no?)

Rest well, till tomorrow. Maybe I will stop by, but it is not definite.

Many, many kisses,

Jaap

Jaap:

The "Kitchen Connection" had to do with the particular, mysterious disappearance of broad beans distributed for sorting by the inmates. Everyone tried to roast them on ashes and near the stoves. Bread was becoming more scarce everyday. People were buzzing near the Central kitchen trying to wheedle a spoonful of gruel from friends in the kitchen. You needed friends in the kitchen to get a little extra food.

———■ ■———

Friday evening, January 7, 1944

My dear love,

It is now 10:10 p.m., but before I go to sleep I want to talk to you for a while.

I know that you are anxious to know the results of my talk with Manja. Yet I cannot really talk about this with you as extensively as you'd like, with me standing on a bench and you lying in your bed. We must therefore wait until you are in good shape again, and then we will chat while taking a peaceful walk.

However, I do want to tell you a few things. On the one hand, Manja showed full understanding for the difficulties we have together; but she emphasized that in Westerbork, a relationship for the three of us, as it stands at the moment, cannot continue. You know that I felt this coming for a long time. In Amsterdam, everything would be a lot easier. You know that we could also make things easier here, but that is a step that I'm not willing to take yet. First of all due to the technical questions of *sperrung*, and secondly, and no less importantly, I would then be tied up with you in more ways than one, which might bring consequences for you which I would not like to have on my conscience. Try to understand, darling, that I'm not trying to back out on you. I hope that you believe that if I were to do this, I would say so openly. But these are things that we will talk about, and if we don't finish, we will in any event write. There is one area in which I will not let you go, and that is in written contact, as crazy as that may sound.

*Sperrung is a German word meaning the stoppage of regular procedure, or exemption from regular German orders and procedures. Any form of protection that was available in the form of lists, special stamps, or favors from the Germans was called Sperrung because it postponed deportation to the East, and possibly meant being saved.

You must also show me that you can be a strong woman for me; meaning that you must keep your chin up.

Manja says that as long as she hears comments about this business, she cannot accept it. And these comments have been unavoidable thus far. She stated that since we came to Westerbork as a married couple, and since we must stay together for the rest of the war, and perhaps even longer; we must at least leave the outside world with an impression of harmony between us; again for our *sperrung*. Now of course, we could meet again "on the sly," but something like that goes against my nature; and I am convinced that the pleasure of these meetings would be eliminated <u>for</u> <u>both</u> <u>of</u> <u>us</u> by the problems they would cause. The peace that we have found with each other until now cannot continue. Once again, we will of course discuss this all (you are probably saying, "<u>how</u> <u>right</u> <u>you</u> <u>are</u>!"), but I have "permission" from Manja to discuss this with you in detail.

I know that you need someone, Ineke, and as much as I love you, I will not be angry if you say "to hell" with all of this. (Of course, you won't say that).

I still believe that something very good could happen between us after the war, but we can't take the chance here in Westerbork against Manja's will.

Sometimes I'm so furious with myself that I, as a married man, as poor as the relationship between Manja and me was and is, could have led a sweet girl like you into this kind of scandal.

It is now 6:00 in the morning: But then I think something good has come out of all this, and if that good gives us both peace in the coming war months, then these months have been victory months. When I look back on the beautiful walks which formed the basis for all we feel for each other, then I feel no regret in having begun this, and I only hope I will also be able to finish it. Of course we will see each other, (and a look at your darling little face is worth a lot to me), but if after all this, you feel that you must put a definite end to it, I will not be angry with you, Ineke.

On the other hand, if you think you can find further happiness with me, then you must try to behave like a strong woman. Only then can I feel at peace, and in all probability, then you will too. Don't talk to anyone about this. I can understand that you would like to talk to someone other than me, but first I want to speak with you myself.

Once again, Manja emphasized that it is absolutely out of the question that the whole camp should know that we might divorce each other; and thus, she cannot tolerate a "second wife" around her.

My darling sweetheart, I find it most unpleasant to hand all these problems to you while you lie sick in bed.

You shall hear more shortly, but here you have the main principles.

I embrace you in my thoughts all the time,

Jaap

Jaap:

It was very disturbing to me to think of the consequences for Ina in our relationship that might occur if it were wholly disclosed to our close community. If it were known that Ina, with her prominent family background, was involved with a poor, married, older man, it would unquestionably have an embarrassing effect on both her and her family.

Ina:

Manja really caused many problems for us which usually coincided with her own sporadic love interests. She made trouble if she didn't have a suitor, even though she knew that she did not wish to remain married to Jaap. If she had a man she was attracted to, she would not bother us at all. We all

45

knew each other, of course, so Manja often felt herself in the midst of an embarrassing situation vis-a-vis the people around us. At awkward times, she strictly forbade us to see each other at all. That was when we would write more often to keep in contact.

———— ■　■ ————

Saturday, January 8, 1944, 1:00 P.M.

My dear girl,

You said this morning that you are sorry that we started all this. Maybe you are right. But on the other hand, we have had so many beautiful times together, and I believe that we both felt it. You can't be sorry about something so beautiful. Would you really be sorry if we continued this way?

We have one thing in common, (of course more than that!), and that is that neither of us takes this kind of thing too lightly. I am a bit older than you, although in experience I am not much older; and I can not make it into a game, because when I start something, it is because I feel it very deeply.

I am dead tired but I really want to finish this letter. I fortunately heard from your mother tonight that you feel a bit better, and that your sister, Josette, is over the worst crisis. Now, physically and mentally stronger, my Ineke will be O.K.

This afternoon I spent an hour at a meeting about Hebrew school; after that to the barrack until 6:00 where I had to do some small chores like shining my shoes; then I ate; then back to school, where Weiss played. He plays technically very well, though not with enough feeling. But to make up for that, Ida Simons-Rosenheimer, who is the best I have ever heard, played. She is a fantastic artist who puts marvelous feelings into her piano playing. I listened to her Thursday night for a half hour, and notwithstanding all the terrible things that are happening, I felt happy.

46

I would have so loved to have spoken to you tonight, but we must learn to accept these absences.

Sleep well, little darling.

My best wishes, and many, many kisses,

Jaap

Ina:

It was heartbreaking for me to say that I was "sorry that we started all this." The ambivalence I felt about our "push-pull" affair was indicative of my feelings of incredulity at finding true love under these most heinous conditions. When I wasn't basking under the warmth of Jaap's protective affection, I would pinch myself to make sure I understood the true meaning of this bizarre situation I found myself in. My youth and inexperience kept me from truly absorbing the depth of my own emotions. But I knew deep down that this was not the time to be stubborn or provocative. We lived in such close quarters, it was important to behave according to the restrictions of the circumstances.

———■   ■———

Monday, January 10, 1944

My dear Ineke,

I am extra busy now because both of the office girls are leaving tomorrow, and the man who keeps the administrative books is sick; so all the work is in front of me. I almost can't get away, not even at 5:30!

I was really happy with your note from this morning, although I sensed the same bad mood in it as in your first letter. I really hope that now you can show me what a strong woman you can be, who will not collapse under the difficult circumstances to come.

Your reaction to Manja's attitude also makes perfect sense; but in spite of this, you must keep it to yourself, as you will no doubt have the good sense to do.

Although our barrack lost the chess match last night, I kept up the honor of our barrack by winning my match. After that we ate with my mother-in-law, then to school, where from 6:30 P.M. till 7:30 P.M. we listened to Ida Simons, who played splendidly, among other things: Beethoven's Moonlight Sonata, a few pieces of Debussy, and finally, a few lovely jazz songs by Peter Kruider and French chansons which she both played and sang, very sweet and multifaceted. We were then at my sister Liesje's for a bit, and then returned to my mother-in-law's, where I read, "The Girl with the Blue Hat" for an hour, completely ridding myself of the irksome mood I was in before. I ended up in bed dead tired, too tired for writing, and I slept until the second whistle.

Tonight more, if I am not too tired. Much, much love,

Jaap

Ina:

Jaap never wanted me to sound like I was losing heart, so he knew how to accept my bad moods without indulging them for too long. He understood better than I how urgent it was for me to act strong, because when I did, I really felt stronger. He was wise enough to know that that was the key to survival.

———— ■ ■ ————

Monday night, January 10, 1944

My dear Ineke,

There is a big hubbub here; everyone is in a pre-transport state of mind.

I think that the list on which you were summoned this afternoon is not so bad. There will be special stamps coming for our papers, and those people who have *Celle and Westerbork on theirs must carefully chose one of the two, which also seems to be a good sign. Thus........ maybe we'll be on transport together!

I have reread both your letters and feel good about the total content. You at least have the courage to look the situation straight in the eye. And the nicest thing was that, in retrospect, you do not feel that the last few months have been a waste of time.

Of course you'll have your bad moods, but then you just take a piece of paper and pour your heart out to me: And if it is a bad letter it doesn't matter, so long as it frees you.

The town of Celle, which was the last station on the trip to Bergen-Belsen, is approximately ten miles from where the camp was located. The name was used interchangeably with the camp name meaning the same place.

Darling, I am going to sleep soon. I trust everything is going well with you.

Many goodnight kisses,

Jaap

Jaap:

Despite the fact that we were in prison, we had freedom to work at assignments, have chess games, concerts, communicate and visit with people. But on Sundays that all changed, because we knew that on that next Tuesday, a train transport would be going out to various "work camps." On Wednesday, we who did not leave on Tuesday breathed a sigh of relief. On Thursday, we started to tremble with terror, because Friday was the day the notices were distributed designating those selected to leave. On Saturday, all those who were chosen worked in a frenzy to change their destiny. Everything was geared to "getting out of transport." Each Tuesday morning at 6 o'clock, the appointed Jewish refugees supervised the loading of the Dutch Jews into the cattle cars. The Germans were using the German Jews to deport the native Dutch Jews from their country.

It was accepted general knowledge that trains left from Westerbork to four destinations: Auschwitz and Sobibor, so-called "work camps;" and Theresienstadt and Bergen-Belsen, so-called "privileged camps." The "work camp" trains, on their way to Poland, were cattle cars with no windows or seating; the Bergen-Belsen and Theresienstadt trains had third class passenger cars. This was one of the few clues that made one destination seem more desirable than another. Also, written word had occasionally been received from certain camps, though none came from Auschwitz. Rumor had it that those in the Polish camps had a very difficult time of it, but no one knew the reality that existed at that time of the extermination camps. We were totally ignorant. It's very hard to realize how little we knew.

Ina:

More than 100 detainees obtained exemptions from the Camp Commandant's office if they had international contacts. They would be going to Bergen-Belsen for exchange purposes. Many who had double options were given a choice of using one or the other. If you had Palestine exchange rights, and you were considered essential to Westerbork, you could remain if you relinquished those rights. Many people chose to risk that, just in case the war ended, or they could discover another means of escaping from being sent to Poland.

Through my father's intervention, my own family had obtained authentic South American documents, in February 1944, which designated us as citizens of El Salvador, and accepted by the Germans as such. However, the notice about the two options applied only to the "Palestine List."

———■ ■———

Wednesday, January 12, 1944

My dearest Ineke,

Another day passed, and this one is an important day for many. It is just after 9:30, and so a perfect time for a peaceful chat with you. I always begin by reading your daily letter. I understand that it is much easier to go through difficult circumstances together; but you must also understand that if we eventually have to take leave of one another, you will have to bear everything by yourself. For although we are together in Westerbork, it indeed might happen that we must leave here.

As to what will happen, we will just have to wait. For the moment, my feelings are good, and hopefully they will stay that way.

I don't feel as good about how pale you looked today. You must try very hard to get well, and if you don't feel completely well, stay in bed an extra day.

I am writing with a pencil stub; hopefully, you can read my almost always illegible handwriting, and figure it out.

So, till tomorrow darling, you sleep well too.

Much, much love,

Jaap

P.S.   One more impression. I had the greatest pleasure in the washroom yesterday morning. I had the perfect opportunity to sneak a look at you–in top form!

Jaap:

Our only bathroom and washroom in the barrack was unisex, and a completely open space with special hours for men and for women to control usage; but in reality, there was very little anyone could do to have any privacy at all. People could walk by outside and peer in at will.

———■ ■———

Thursday afternoon, January 13, 1944

My dear sweetheart,

It is dead quiet here. My bosses have gone to pray. I was happy with your note, because I see from it that you feel the same as I do about our little talks. It is as if in these few minutes we can at least bring each other up to date on the very small things, too insignificant to write about, but fun to tell. I am glad that you don't have to go to work again before Monday. Try to get a good rest before then: maybe we can have our usual chatting hour on Monday or Tuesday night.

There really isn't any more news to tell, just as you had none for me. Not that there isn't any news, or that no news is being made. But I'm taking it all very calmly with the remark: "I have to see it first."

In any event, the most important thing is that we are not on this coming Tuesday's transport. We probably won't have to disappoint the people that we invited over for Saturday evening, so that should still take place. Tonight, despite my better intentions, I won't see you, as my mother-in-law is in Barrack 83. My thoughts still are always with you, and in these thoughts I send you many, many kisses, and love,

Jaap

Jaap:

Of course, "entertaining" was only possible in a very limited way in Westerbork. However, there were a number of cottages inhabited by the original German Jewish residents where it was possible to receive people.

Manja's mother briefly stayed in one of the cottages, thereby gaining access for me and Manja.

———— ■ ■ ————

Friday, January 14, 1944

My dearest Ineke,

It is now Friday afternoon, 5 o'clock , and my "bosses' are having a talk with Our Lord. You already know the political news of the *IPA*, so we are in all probability sitting here on the wrong side like the Russians, not to mention the English. My optimism about our "list" has also dwindled, due to a report I received this afternoon. But that could also mean nothing. We must wait and see. Tomorrow we will go on as planned; we don't want to disappoint the people even though we don't feel good about it at all.

I thought you looked a little healthier today: Continue that way, and in any case, try to get as much rest as possible. You don't know what will happen if we have to go elsewhere. (And I don't mean Portugal, where we would have a splendid little life!) What you wrote to me about Manja's lack of consent to our little chats, I really don't think that it was meant that we should have even less contact

*The IPA , International Palestine Agency, was the acronym facetiously referred to by the Jews who brought war news into camp through outside contacts. Sometimes they were just rumors, but they usually had some basis in fact. They were always eagerly awaited and received by inmates of the camp.

than normal people in our barrack would. So I really don't feel guilty about such glimpses of each other; actually I feel quite good!

We will no doubt be meeting in our barrack in the evening, because our little cottage "49" has been taken away from us as long as my mother-in-law is in the hospital. Tonight, I am going to play gin rummy, (that is something I also like to do) with my friend Han who has the mail table at his disposal, where we can at least sit properly.

Sleep extra well and peacefully, and dream of people you love.

Many, many kisses,

Jaap

Jaap:

As usual, Friday at sundown brought the start of the Jewish Sabbath.

The mention of Portugal referred to the "Weinreb Protection" promising safe passage to Portugal for Manja and me which we had also purchased. The "Weinreb List," in spite of being the complete hoax that it was, actually postponed deportation for many people, thus giving them that extra few months' difference in helping them to survive.

—————■   ■—————

Saturday, January 15, 1944, 10:10 P.M.

My darling,

There is a small possibility that we have to go to Theresienstadt this coming Tuesday, of course as a "favor." You can well understand how I feel, but we have weighed all the pros and cons, and have decided that we cannot refuse an offer such as this. Our "Weinreb Protection," according to my sister-in-law, is not 100% valid; and she is very much afraid that she will not be able to get us out of the next Auschwitz transport. Theresienstadt is at least something concrete, assuming that they will let us young people leave. And maybe the "Weinreb" will turn out to be good. Then we might be able to leave from Theresienstadt, in which case we would have our "protection" papers given to us there. Also, we could obtain an eventual Palestine Certificate, which we expect would be forwarded to Theresienstadt, as this is the only Jewish camp with which there is a regular contact. And finally, there is a motive for Manja, namely, that she gets to go with her mother, *who in any event* has to go on transport; and if she doesn't go with us, she has no chance, and will go to Auschwitz. Despite everything, (and in this case, you happen to be everything), I do believe that if I get this chance I must not reject it as we have nothing outside of "Weinreb"; and therefore, I might have to go on transport in cattle cars with the 900 Punishment Cases: not a very appealing prospect. You know I am an optimist, but I really think that there is a serious possibility of this happening. In higher circles, the "Weinreb" is not yet taken seriously.

I am writing in record time, so also in record illegibility, the reason being that I am afraid that the lights will go out at any moment!

There are 3 possibilities. First of all that it doesn't work, then nothing happens.

Secondly, that it works, and then we will have to leave on Tuesday.

The third chance is that I still could be put on the "1,000 list." (Don't fret!) There is a chance that Manja and I can have two places that will fall vacant. Rabbi Frank was really very appreciative of my work here, and promised to try his best to help. It is even possible that if I am called for transport next Tuesday I'll be able to get out of it; and if it is possible, I'll be put on the "1,000 list." The latter I cannot believe at this moment. My darling, you mustn't let all this worry your little head. That doesn't help anything; and whatever will be, will be.

If I go, we will no doubt see each other before; and if I don't go, it's even better. If I go, I already have a last will and testament, (in the good sense of the word!) for you, which I am still working on. Hopefully, it won't be needed. Don't talk to anyone about it, not even at tonight's "party"–lights out–Sunday morning more.

Our musical evening was very successful: A large mixture of people dominated by women, with a big pot of coffee on our school stove. Before the intermission, a classical program with dances by Brahms and Schubert, then a Bach Violin Concerto (in 2 parts). Then came some beautiful folk songs. So we, and all our guests felt uplifted.

Tomorrow morning in school, we will have a lecture from 10:30 A.M. - 11:30 A.M. by Sam Dresden about French Literature; and from 11:30 - 12:30 P.M., Professor Cohen will give a talk about Ancient History. If our new plans don't interfere, we hope to go further with this.

Again, don't worry, spirits up.!

In my thoughts, many, many kisses.

Jaap

Jaap:

The "1,000 list" was created in Westerbork on September 9, 1943, by the Commandant, giving preferential treatment to the Dutch Jews for the first time. Most of the people listed were workers in the metal industry; and everyone on the list understood it allowed them to extend their stay in Westerbork . I counted on getting a place on the list because of my work with the school.

The 900 Punishment Cases were treated very harshly. They were made to sleep with five people to three beds placed together–all 900 jammed together in one hut. It would sometimes take two hours for someone's turn in the washroom.

Professor David Cohen was one of the two heads of the Amsterdam Jewish Council, and had been Professor of Ancient History and Roman Antiquities at the City University of Amsterdam. I knew him to be a wonderful speaker, very well-known, and he represented the best of Dutch Jewry. Although not everyone would agree, I think he tried to do the best he could as President of the Jewish Council.

———■   ■———

Sunday, January 16, 1944

My dear girl,

Just a few more words, although it is already 10:10 P.M., which is very late after this emotional night and day. I am totally exhausted. How glad I am that I can stay here, you can't imagine. After each transport there is a severing of ties; and we don't know if they'll ever be repaired, no matter how optimistic I am. But at least we have weathered another storm.

I am too tired to convey my thoughts.

So darling, excuse me for these few words. Tomorrow, more. Sleep well.

Many, many goodnight kisses,

Jaap

———■   ■———

Monday night, 9:45, January 17, 1944

My dear sweetheart,

Just now I witnessed *Rabbi Goldberg's* emotional departure, with a wonderful speech by your Papa. I really thought I was going to run into you this afternoon, as I had a meeting with your boss's husband regarding his leadership of Barrack 39. Mrs. Wilzig kept on talking to me, and although I think she would have liked to discuss other subjects than the next transport, she didn't dare to.

This afternoon I was at school until 6:30 P.M. Later, Manja came to school where we can cook a hot meal, and we took advantage of this and ate there. Tonight, I also went to the hospital for a while, then a few departure visits, then Goldberg's departure. So you have a chronological report of the day in Westerbork, the same as on so many other days.

Rabbi Goldberg was the first school principal in Westerbork.

59

More important than this, is that we can still stay here together, even though we cannot be together. Your letter made me feel very good, as it showed that you feel exactly as I do.

Tomorrow night, I really hope to talk about all this with you; it will be much better than writing. We will discuss the time tomorrow afternoon. If you don't feel completely O.K., however, tell me, and be honest. Darling, think about me as much and as nicely as I think about you; then all is well. Many, many goodnight kisses.

Jaap

Ina:

Westerbork was like a nightmarish, make-believe world. One day you were sick with fear; the next day you were at a concert listening to some of the world's greatest artists. We had one of the best hospitals in the camp, and the best doctors were there practicing, so they never believed they would come to any harm. The "cream" of the intellectual elite in the Dutch Jewish population all passed through Westerbork. They thought a work camp would be another Westerbork. They worked as normally as possible, all awaiting the relentless deportations.

———■ ■———

Wednesday night, 10:00, January 19, 1944

My dear Ineke,

Tonight, I greeted you and you greeted me from a distance. Just as mine, your mood tonight was one of laughter, not of tears, despite the fact that you looked very bad, really dead tired. Hopefully, you will feel better by the time you receive this. It's so hectic here in the office, as we are about to start teaching in the *school again, and of course taking care of Manja too, for which she is truly grateful, making it at least nicer for me. Hopefully, we will be speaking soon. Sweetheart, more tomorrow; now I am going to sleep, till tomorrow.

Many, many kisses,

Jaap

———■　■———

Thursday night, January 20, 1944, 10:15 P.M.

My sweet girl,

How did you like our walk from the hospital tonight? Very amusing, no? It is crazy, but every day I have so many thoughts that I want to convey to you, but when evening comes, my brain doesn't work anymore, and I can't remember. In the future, I am going to make notes.

Maybe we can have a talk tomorrow night too. Don't think I'd planned on seeing you. Of course I would have wished it, but it seems that fate takes care of our meetings. You wrote in your last letter that I mustn't joke about "making a big scene" with Manja. You are absolutely right, and I don't think I was completely honest about it. As long as the relationship between Manja and me stays the same, quite good, both of us are satisfied. Only I am always thinking

*Every week after transport, when so many children and teachers were sent away, the school had to be closed then reopened, and reorganized for the new arrivals.

61

about the third party, about my Ineke. Hopefully, we will talk about it soon. Sleep sweetly.

Much love,
Jaap

———■ ■———

Saturday night, January 22, 1944, 9:45 P.M.

My dear Ineke,

As always, I was glad for your note, especially because you got rid of your bad mood, hopefully, for a long time. I saw it this morning on your face! In the meantime, you also received your official "Weinreb" listing. Hopefully, this will lead to our attaining our goal. I had a very calm day today. I read and finished "Professor Bernardi" by Schnitzler. Very clever, but I never much liked reading plays; even now. They are really something you should see.

Are you coming to the lectures tomorrow morning at school? I think that I'm only going to Sam Dresden's lecture, as I have to work afterwards.

The first whistle is now blowing, so if I stop now, I will be asleep by the second whistle. Sweet darling, stay as strong as I thought you sounded in your letter. Then everything will come out fine: hopefully, quickly.

Sleep sweetly, and well,
Much, much love,
Jaap

Ina:

Sometimes I did not reveal to Jaap that what he had called my 'bad mood' was really a lack of physical well being. He worried so intensely about me that I preferred for him to think that I was in a 'bad mood'. But this time I was feeling much better physically, so I guess it was reflected in my face and in my letter. I was really determined to rise above our worries and uncertainties, and prove to myself and Jaap that I could be strong in the face of adversity.

———■ ■———

Sunday night, January 23, 1944, 10:00 P.M.

My dearest sweet girl,

Just a little gossip with you before I go to sleep. I was away from the barrack today for one hour, and so I didn't get to see your pretty face. First, I went to my mother-in-law's where I peacefully read a detective book, (a special hobby of mine), by Havank. After that I stayed and ate, and then to school where I stoked the fire for our music night. The fire was going, but it went out when I wasn't looking. I was not cut out by nature to be a fire stoker! The evening itself was a great success. Only one thing was a pity. (You yourself must fill in what!). Bea and Herta played again; Millie played a few parts of Violin Concertos by Bach and Winiawski. The latter was especially good. Then there was a Russian singer with his own guitar and songs; very lovely, and Mrs. Elias sang Viennese songs, also with a guitar. Finally, and best of all was Ida Simons. The Soep family was present in the person of your Aunt. Now I am going to sleep, for as usual, I am dead tired. Hopefully, you also had a nice and peaceful day. Till tomorrow, darling. Sleep tight,

Many, many kisses,

Jaap

———■ ■———

Monday evening, January 24, 1944, 9:30 P.M.

My darling,

Finally, I am a little early, but I also had to leave work early to see what my chances were for the Transport Service. The day before the transport is always somewhat nervewracking; the worst is, that due to the impression left by the cattle cars, my thoughts about my Father and Mother won't leave my head. To think that they have already been gone for half a year!

It is of course, very sad about Noorje, especially because she was the first to get rid of the S-Badge. If she hadn't been let out of the Penal Barrack, we wouldn't have known any better, but now it feels different. On the other hand, you must look at it in the same way I look at our imminent departure: that is, that 90,000 Jews from the Netherlands have already had to bear this, then why not us, especially since we are young. (If I can include myself with my bald head!)

School starts again next Thursday, which will give me an unbelievably heavy work load. Hopefully, this work will put me on the "1,000 list" but maybe I shouldn't hope for that. I don't know anymore. Till tomorrow when I see you. Hopefully, you are feeling much better.

Much, much love,

Jaap

Jaap:

I was part of a Jewish group of workers enlisted by the Germans to help the *OD*, harsh and brutal German Jews in charge of putting deportees on the train. On transport duty, we helped carry luggage, find places for the elderly, the sick, and the children on the trains, and tried to assuage some of the fears of those leaving. It was a sickening, wrenching experience that I will never forget. Most of the good-byes were final ones.

I recall my parents' deportation in July, 1943: After I knew they were going on transport, I visited with them and helped them pack. While packing, I saw that my father's shoes weren't in great shape, and I said, "Why don't you take my shoes? You have the same size, and you will be working hard and need good shoes". I accompanied them to the train the next morning and bid them what we later learned was a **final farewell*.

———■ ■———

*OD in German, Ordnungs Dienst, means Order Service.
**Frederik and Grietje Polak were killed in the gas chambers at Sobibor a few days later. Jaap's words last spoken to his father are etched on one of the six glass pillars of the Holocaust Memorial in the center of the city of Boston, Massachusetts.

Tuesday, January 25, 1944

My dear girl,

Just before I go to sleep, another little chat with you. I think I am as tired as you usually are. This morning at the transport, I had to do dirty work. Dirty in every sense of the word. Things like this take so much out of you emotionally, that you can well understand that I want to go directly to sleep.

That your friend Noortje's departure has gotten you down makes perfect sense. Every departure gets us down, as each one means another transport. But now this transport is over, and as things are, we must go on. You also, darling, until the next week. That is how we all live here. About our letter yesterday, I will get back to it when I am less tired. For now, you must do with these simple lines.

With the opening of school, it looks as if the office will be in a bad situation. To think I am now head of it all. I did have a chance to accompany Professor Franck to the cattle car today where I found a small place for him.

Dear lady, in my thoughts I kiss you. Until tomorrow,

Jaap

———■　■———

Wednesday night, January 26, 1944, 10:15 P.M.

My dear Ineke,

As I told you, I am pretty busy, and I even had to work tonight. I ran into Josette while still at school where she was at a Hachshara meeting.

I thought you looked a little peaked today. I hope my little lady doesn't worry too much? I don't see you going to Celle yet, but that is based mostly on feelings; hopefully, these feelings aren't wrong. In the meantime, nothing is known about the next transport.

Your letters, as usual, are great, just as if we are really talking. But I am not at all satisfied with my letters, although you know that I am basically not a letter writer. This way you only get to know my bad side.

Much, much love,
Jaap

Ina:

Hachshara is the Hebrew name for the training program for people whose goal it was to go to Israel to work on the land. Before the Nazi invasion, there had been a large group of German Hachshara members, young men and women working in different areas of Holland, where they were trained for agriculture, horticulture, housekeeping, and animal husbandry. When the Nazis closed the work villages, Dutch families took these young boys and girls into their homes. My family took one in, and so did my brother Benno; that's how he was killed: in a raid, the Germans, using a list of all the Hachshara people, took Benno, together with the young pioneer, out of his home.

■   ■

Thursday night, January 27, 1944, 9:45 P.M.

My dearest girl,

I was at the barrack for a moment around 6:00, really only to see your pretty face, but unfortunately, you weren't there. Now I have to make do with just a pencil. Everyone is fully occupied with what might happen this coming Tuesday, but as to that you know my feeling. I had a call today to come to the Visa Station; and I thought *with fear* that there was a Palestine Certificate for us (which in that case would mean that we would have to leave this coming Tuesday). But fortunately, all they needed was information about my sister, Betty, and her husband, who are on the "5th list."

Yes sweetheart, if you say that in this way we don't get to be close enough to each other, it is true, and it used to be the opposite; but we must make the best of a bad situation. Maybe, in this way, we will be able to find out if what we have between us is a good basis for what eventually will be for life. I know that this is a lot easier for me to put on paper than it is for you to do, but please keep your chin up.

Sleep sweetly. Many, many kisses,

Jaap

Jaap:

Betty Polak, my middle sister, went underground throughout the war, active in the Resistance movement, taking different identities in order to perform her duties. She had married Flip de Leeuw before the war, who was an economist, very Zionist-minded, and an officer in the Dutch Army when Holland was invaded. However, in 1943, both Betty and Flip were caught, accused of involvement in the blowing up of a train. Although the Germans killed her husband, Betty proved through false papers that she was neither involved with this man, nor a Jew, and continued her covert work throughout the war.

Ina:

Yes, I did complain about our separation sometimes, but I guess I had come to need Jaap and his dependable support and love more than I realized. He became my beacon of strength, and I began to rely on that strength more and more as time wore on.

———■ ■———

Friday night, January 28, 1944, 9:45 P.M.

Dearest Ineke,

First of all, I was glad to hear from Josette that your fever was down. Hopefully, you will have a speedy recovery, although you will have to miss the lectures this weekend.

I had a real unlucky day. Very busy at school, a leak in the stove, which gave me a lousy headache, and then at 6:15, I fell into a pothole full of water, and although I didn't hurt myself, I did have to go back and change clothes. But then I got a letter from you, and when I talk with you, everything becomes rosy, and my bad mood disappears like snow in the sun. There isn't much news here, besides all the "IPA's" about the next transport. We have a new advisor in our barrack, one of my sister-in-law's German-Jewish bosses, and you can understand that I think it's great, as it can only be good for my position. He has a reputation for being one of the best. Only I don't see much good coming from the "1,000 list".

Now darling, I hope that you will be OK very soon.

Have happy dreams, From Jaap who gives you many, many kisses in his thoughts, without fear of catching any germs from you! With a real lousy pencil stub, this is more illegible than usual!

Jaap:

The "1,000 list" now consisted mostly of people in the metal industry, to which Manja belonged.

Hans Hanauer was one of the heads of the German-Jewish hierarchy that helped run Westerbork. Hans had a reputation of being the most decent of them. Manja's sister was Hanauer's secretary, which was quite a good job; eventually, he helped her to be sent to Theresienstadt, where she survived the war.

——■   ■——

Saturday night, January 29, 1944, 10:15 P.M.

My dear girl,

How annoying that you don't feel well. I hope you get better soon. My throat is beginning to do strange things, but I still feel good, so I hope that tomorrow I can swallow normally again. Today, after you saw me, I slept 1½ hours, then went to my mother-in-law, ate there, then to the hospital to see an uncle of mine, and a few acquaintances of Manja's. Finally, I got to Be's lecture, which was very good, and where the only thing I regretted was that I didn't see your face. So you have a chronological report of this day, which was really much more unnerving than it sounds in view of the coming transport.

Sweet darling, I am not satisfied with this letter at all, but my intentions are good.

Much, much love,

Jaap

——■   ■——

Ina:

I was asthmatic even as a child, but the really bad attacks started when deportations began. When my boyfriend, Rudi, was arrested, I had one attack that lasted for three months. So when I was exposed to all the elements at Westerbork that gave everyone else colds and sore throats with continuing coughing, sneezing and wheezing, I was not surprised that my own illnesses were exacerbated. There was constant dampness in the barracks, drafts coming through the doors which were open and shut all day long, water condensation on the roof which dripped down in many areas, and bare, uneven, wooden planks roughly nailed together that were the walls of the barracks through which the cold winds whipped.

One night, I had a high fever and sore throat, and the next day I was informed that I had contracted diphtheria. I was brought to the hospital and placed in quarantine in the Isolation Barrack, a large ward of diphtheria patients. They administered the appropriate serum to counteract the infection so the throat swelling would recede, and I remained there for a long siege. No one was permitted to see me except through a window of the hospital barrack which was also enclosed by a fence. Jaap used to stand outside and call, and I would come to the window and see him so we could talk.

After about a week into the illness, the horse-serum cure brought on the so called "serum sickness". It was one of the most debilitating illnesses I ever went through. Every day, another symptom appeared, like large blisters on the body, unbearable itching, intestinal upsets, and generally feeling deathly sick. Eventually, it all passed, but I still had to stay in the Isolation Barrack for six weeks with my fellow patients.

———■　■———

Tuesday morning, February 1, 1944, 8:45 A.M.
My dearest Ineke,

Although we had the morning off, I still went to the office, as it is such a mess in the barrack with so many people whom I can't help. It is wonderfully quiet here, and the others aren't coming in till 9:00; so I have at least 15 minutes to talk with you in the peaceful way that we are used to, that we like so much. Last night I spoke with Josette, at which time we mainly discussed the problem of who will now be the Messenger of Love. It is less of a problem for me, as I can deliver my letters to a courier who is on our side. For your part, it is probably best that you save your letters which is not nice for me, but at least that way I will receive a kind of diary from you. Then you can have your letters delivered a couple of times a week in closed envelopes, which I will send you tomorrow from school without a sender's name on them. In this way, I think that we will be able to avoid future difficulties. Of course I don't like that we have to do it this way, but I see no better solution, without involving too many other people. On the one hand, maybe it is good that Josette goes on transport (although I mean it kindly), because if she keeps on being the messenger, things could go bad quickly. She is very talkative, and I am worried that she may tell the wrong people about us.

I understand completely that you might have moments of doubt about my "loyalty" to you. I, of course, have the same feelings, also caused by the fact that we have no direct contact anymore; and that the relationship with Manja is good again. But that is no reason to despair that all the happiness we had will not return. This we will also find out in time. But there is one thing that you must think about; that even if, later, we don't see each other again, you should look back on that which we had together as something very special, and that should give you strength later in your life. Maybe, and it is quite possible, you are not at all satisfied with what I wrote here; as in it, you don't find everything you would like to read. I promised you however, that I would always be honest, and you should also not think that I love you less than before. On the contrary! On the other hand, I don't want to tie you down, because you are in reality, free.

My sweet darling, I must stop now, and I am not at all satisfied with what I wrote; but it is so hard for me to talk about these difficult things in writing. I hope that we can find a quiet corner where we can talk this over really well.

My dear girl, keep well, and think as many good things about me as I do about you.

Much, much love and kisses,

Jaap

P.S. After finishing this letter, even after I sealed it shut, I got some free time without people around me, to tell you some day-to-day things. First of all, Han Maykels and his mother were called for transport last night at 12:30, which was bad this late. *The sixth list is definitely free from this transport, which is very reassuring for us. I tell you honestly that I am now convinced that both of us will end up in Bergen-Belsen. They are now saying that the next Bergen-Belsen transport will be on February 22. Of course you will not be able to go on that transport because of your illness, but I hope to see you on the transport after that. Before that, something special could happen. People from Amsterdam are talking "big" about the coming

---

*The "sixth list" was known officially as the 6th Veteran Zionist List on immigration into Palestine for exchange.

invasion. I have to see it before I believe it. Some of the others on the "sixth list" who will go along with me on the transport are many that I know. Yesterday, I paid some visits to the barrack where everyone was nervous. I think Josette agrees that it's good to go now, and honestly I must say I feel good about it too. I am slowly beginning to believe the good things I hear about Bergen-Belsen; and I believe that everyone with a "120,000 diamond list" stamp will go to Palestine. Dear girl of mine, I think that I gave you enough to read. Till tomorrow,

Jaap

———— ■   ■ ————

Wednesday, February 2, 1944, 6:00 P.M.

My beautiful girl,

Despite my words from yesterday as to whether Josette should play postman, I am truly glad that she wormed her way out of the transport. I will tell her to be a bit careful and not so loud about it; in that case, she's really the best person to continue doing it.

It was nice to see you with a little color. It's the opposite with me, probably because I am dead tired and have a headache, caused by how busy it was at school and with that filthy heater in the office. Last night, as I told you, I went to bed early, (for me quite an achievement), at 8:00 P.M., and I fell asleep in a minute, so I probably needed it. A transport such as this brings with it a lot of emotions and fatigue. I brought my Uncle Joe Asscher and my friend Han Maykels to the train, and boldly walked ahead so I could at least go to the front of the train to say my many goodbyes, although I am not a man who likes to say goodbye. I didn't have Transport Service this time because only the "73" and "85 lists" were called. On the other hand, the goodbyes this time weren't too sad as we expect to follow shortly. However, now I think that it will take a little longer. My sister, Liesje, thought it was great to be going. But you can understand that, because of those whose final destination is Palestine, it is just a step along the way. I made good use of the vacancies to take another bed, very close to my bed, near Van den Bergh and Jaap, with whom we have morning and midday meals. I just looked for books for you and I found this one by Conan Doyle which looks suitable for you, although I may be completely wrong. Tonight, I don't have any special plans. Only I think that we should slowly ready our belongings, as in any event we will have to move. So, Manja and I, right after the transport train left, started to look over the things in our rucksacks and trunk. We're very glad that we did it, and after two hours of work, we now know what we have, or better said, what we don't have. My dear, I really must stop as it is now 6:30 P.M.; and I hope I have at least given you something to read in your sickbed, even if it is nothing too special.

Please be strong, my little lady,

Much, much love,

Jaap

——■ ■——

Thursday night, February 3, 1944, 6:15 P.M.

My dearest girl,

Again a day passed. This time, as so many times before a very nervewracking day. The worst part for me, was that against my intentions, I found no opportunity to visit you, as I had to wait at school for Rabbi Frank who came at around 5:45 P.M. As you of course have already heard, they canceled the "Weinreb List". I just got the official written notice which I'm sure you will get any moment now. First of all, this is a complete disaster for my mother-in-law because that was her only protection, so you can understand how Manja feels. Furthermore, our own business is not in order yet either, as our official papers from the "Palestine List" still haven't come in from Amsterdam; and as long as they aren't in, we can't put in any Official Requests, and are in fact without protection. Of course, in special cases something can be done, for which I will approach Rabbi Frank; and Manja would go to her group leader, so that two parties would be working to get us out of this transport. In addition, my sister-in-law is keeping a sharp eye on things for us. All in all, I am not so afraid for us, but on the other hand, we also want to do everything we can to prevent unexpected things from happening. For my mother-in-law, it is much more difficult. The only possibility would be to get her onto our certificate, which might be possible, because on the registration number pages it states "Family Jacob Polak," to which she could belong. But we really must wait and see how all this develops. This *Weinreb situation has happened quite suddenly. You know that my feelings about it have been quite good up until now, and now it appears that my feelings were good for nothing. For people who have nothing else, it is disastrous.

As I told you, I felt very bad that I didn't get to visit you. Tomorrow, I really hope to do better, providing that nothing happens, and I will try to get away.

As to the weather, you really don't have to regret that you can't go out. You are better off in bed.

How is the book that I sent you? It was the only English fiction novel I could find; and although it is only a detective story, I hope you liked it.

---

*Thousands of people who had relied on the "Weinreb List" to help them evade deportation to Auschwitz had their hopes cruelly smashed for them. Although there was much skepticism from the beginning about the ultimate benefit of the "List," even by Weinreb himself, it was an anchor that many people clung to, nevertheless. It ended up as a bizarre hoax that only served to deepen the fears of so many helpless people who truly had nothing else to believe in.

Just take care that your health stays as it is now, and then I will be satisfied. And eat as well as you can as you need it.

Much, much love, kisses, etc.....

Jaap

Jaap:

Manja's group leader in the clothing industry where she worked in Westerbork, had been very important in the same business before the war. This industry, where clothes were taken apart for fabric, and pieced goods were stitched together, the recycling of fabrics, was important work in Westerbork; and there was a chance that this work could keep Manja and me in the camp.

———■　■———

Friday night, February 4, 1944, 6:00 P.M.

My dear girl,

This time another written letter, mostly because the Sabbath just started. They are starting the service next door; so it's difficult for me to use the typewriter. For the first time in a long time, Our Good Lord, hopefully just for today(!) was not with us. I was in front of your barrack where I guess you didn't hear my whistle because of the storm, so I went back to my barrack without success. Nothing to be done. Maybe I'll come again Saturday or Sunday, but I doubt I can. So you must concentrate on the fact that even though we are separated from each other by quite a distance, we at least have close written contact.

Rabbi Frank will give me an answer tomorrow. I really hope he can do something; and what is most important is that tomorrow they will propose to the German command that all the people on the "6th list" should be privileged to stay in Westerbork. As there are only 30 of us, we have a chance.

Last evening we didn't really do anything special. We ate in the barrack, as the "49" was too crowded again. In all probability we will keep eating here, though it is far from a pleasure, as the kind of people in the barrack are the worst. Even my mother-in-law had a row with one of the new people. After that, I visited my friend, Nystad who is being released with his family to go to Barneveld.

In the meantime, the weather has gotten worse. The wind almost swept me away when I went from "64" to school. Tomorrow, I will have a half-hour rest from 1:30 P.M. until 2:00 P.M., which will give me a chance to talk to you. Now I'll stop, because I have nothing more to write. Think of me when the whistle blows. This will then be mutual. An extra Sabbath kiss, and much love,

Jaap

Jaap:

There had been an onslaught of new people arriving in the barracks–less educated, and from a lower socio-economic class, who were creating havoc for the previous residents with their raucous, rowdy behavior.

Barneveld was a castle in the East of Holland originally set up as an internment camp for some of the more prominent Jewish intelligentsia of The Netherlands. Recently, a group of inmates from Barneveld had arrived at Westerbork with the guarantee of being sent to Theresienstadt, another so-called "privileged" camp in Czechoslovakia set up for artists and intellectuals. However, we learned later that many of the Theresienstadt inmates were sent to Auschwitz anyway.

———— ■ ■ ————

Saturday afternoon, February 5, 1944

My dear, sweet darling,

Our Good Lord was not with us this time, as I had planned to visit you between 12:00 and 12:30; but it was impossible for me, as I had some urgent business to tend to regarding our "protection". The matter seems to be for the most part in good order for us. For the moment, I am not nervous about it, and.......I trust you weren't either. Rabbi Frank was here this morning to tell me that he had taken care of our Protection Visa for the week; and moreover, that Manja can finally stay here on her Industry Paper. Also, the papers for the "Palestine List" might come in before the next transport arrives. Things also look more favorable for my mother-in-law; thus I hope that everything will work out.

It is still a big mess in our barrack. Last night, one of the barrack leaders gave a speech, in which he said that although nothing had been stolen here in the beginning, in the last few days, many people have lost things. (I heard everything from other people, as I was asleep and no one woke me up.) I slept even better in my new quarters than I did in my previous top bunk.

Tonight, Dr. Van der Waal from the Barneveld barrack will give a lecture on "The Romantic in Painting", with a slide projector in the big room at the orphanage. In addition, tomorrow we will have lectures in the usual public room, and tomorrow afternoon, there will be a lecture on "Sociology in Judaism". In this way, my weekend is somewhat full. If I could fit a visit to the hospital into that program...I cannot tell you how much I want to; although I can't say for sure that I will, and I am sorry about that. So we must wait and see. This has been going on for so long now.

The typewriter ribbon has given up, so therefore, these final words in pencil, not too much, as I have no further news, but you can understand why I need pencils.

Hopefully, you will be *negative for the second time!

Dear child, all the best, hold your head up.

Many, many kisses

Jaap

> *Jaap*:
>
> A giant blast of bad news came down on the camp that day that had never occurred before:
>
> All the exemption stamps belonging to hospital patients were suddenly declared invalid. The only exemptions to be honored were the Barnevelders; those on the "1,000 List", partners from mixed marriages, and the baptized. All others would have to prepare to leave on the transport to Auschwitz next Tuesday. No exceptions were allowed, even for those who were still ill. Ina was included in this group.

Negative refers to a medical test for the presence of diphtheria virus. Three negatives meant that one was cured.

Ina:

Can anyone ever imagine the abject terror I felt when I heard this news? But I did not panic. I had the utmost confidence in my father's assurances that he would try to "fix" it. Then, too, I had Jaap's strength backing me. His love was like a warm, protective wall against all the misery I was enduring. How much strength I derived just from knowing he was there for me!

———■　■———

Sunday morning, February 6, 1944, 10:30 A.M.

My dearest Ineke,

You can understand all our fears and feelings from yesterday's bad and miserable news. In the beginning of the evening, I spoke to your father who really didn't say much; but later, I spoke with Josette who told me exactly what has been done, and that calmed me down. So you see that your father is really doing everything he can; you can be sure of it. There is no doubt that there will be some people taken out of the transport; and it would really be almost impossible for you not to be one of them, especially since you are only one person which is very, very important with each transport. I really do not have the contacts your father has, so I trust he will be able to take care of it. In case something should go wrong, then I will of course immediately go to see what I can do via my contacts with the Jewish Council; but I really believe that there will be no need for that. It is especially lousy now, because we haven't seen each other for so many days. I will try to pass by tomorrow morning between 11:30 and 12:00 A.M., so look out for me. Although neither Manja nor I felt like going to a lecture, we went to hear van der Waal last night, really only to get out for a while, because you go crazy in the barrack from the many and bad stories you hear from everyone. The lecture was boring, though the contents not uninteresting. The only lively note was brought up by Professor Kisch with the question, "How come that in music and literature of the Romantic Period there is always talk about night and the darker side of life, while in Romantic Painting and Sculpture everything is in a more pleasant light?" Whereupon the Professor himself commented that a book or piano piece absorbs your time for only a few hours, while you must look at a painting for a lifetime. The artists were looking for what would sell well. A completely materialistic solution!

I hope you sleep as well in the hospital as you did here in the barrack, where you were in comparatively close proximity to me.

Now I am at school, where lessons are in progress on the other side. I still have a lot of work to do, but this is the beginning of my labors.

My darling, this is all for the moment. The best thing here in Westerbork is when there is no news; as all news is bad news. Do you believe that there are moments that I hope that my "Palestine Certificate" will send me to Celle, even if it means saying goodbye to you for a few weeks. Of course then, my second wish is that you come with your "120,000" stamp right after me, or even better, in the same train. Maybe that will happen faster than we think.

Dearest lady, spirits up, everything will be all right; I am still thinking about you. Maybe that will help you a little.

Many, many kisses,

Jaap

———■　■———

JAAP POLAK'S MOTHER AND FATHER, GRIETJE AND FREDERIK POLAK
ENGAGEMENT PHOTO, EARLY 1900'S.

INA SOEP'S PARENTS, TONI FREDERIKA AND ABRAHAM
SOEP IN CANNES, 1946.

JAAP POLAK WITH TWO OF HIS SISTERS, BETTY, CENTER,
AND JUUL, 1921.

INA SOEP AND YOUNGER SISTER,
JOSETTE, AS BRIDESMAIDS, 1930.

BENNO SOEP, INA'S BROTHER WITH INA, CENTER, AND
SISTER, JOSETTE, 1932.

MENU

ter gelegenheid van het
BARMITSWOFEEST
van

JACOB POLAK
VRIJDAGAVOND

23 TEIWEIS 5686
8 JANUARI 1926

Hors d'Oeuvre

❖

Kippensoep

❖

Gevogelte met Compôte

❖

Tuinboontjes met Tong

❖

Diverse Groenten met Kalfsvleesch

❖

IJspudding

❖

Dessert

❖

JAAP POLAK ON HIS BAR MITZVAH DAY WITH THE CELEBRATORY DINNER MENU INCLUDING:
CHICKEN SOUP, POULTRY WITH STEWED FRUITS, FAVA BEANS WITH TONGUE, VEAL WITH ASSORTED VEGETABLES, AND ICE PUDDING (SIMILAR TO ICE CREAM). DESSERT WAS COOKIES, PETIT FOURS AND OTHER SWEETS.

INA WITH HER SWEETHEART, RUDI ACOHEN, WHO DIED IN AUSCHWITZ IN 1942.

RUDI ACOHEN AT AGE 18, 1940.

WEARING JEWISH STARS, INA, LEFT, DANCING WITH FRIENDS. RUDI IS IN THE CENTER

JAAP POLAK'S FATHER, FREDERIK POLAK, WITH EYEGLASSES, THIRD FROM LEFT IN REAR, IN THE COMPANY OF CHAIM WEIZMANN, EXTREME LEFT, AND VLADIMIR JABOTINSKY, RIGHT, AT THE CONVENTION OF THE PALESTINE FOUNDATION FUND, THE FIRST ORGANIZATION TO RAISE FUNDS FOR PALESTINE IN HOLLAND, AT THE CONCERTGEBOUW IN AMSTERDAM. 1921.

JAAP POLAK IS IN THE CENTER OF HIS ZIONIST GROUP, 1936.

ABRAHAM SOEP, INA'S FATHER, A
MEMBER OF THE JEWISH COUNCIL,
WEARING HIS YELLOW STAR, 1942.

BENJ. A. SOEP & Cº.,

ROUGH AND POLISHED DIAMONDS
MANUFACTORY AND OFFICES

NIEUWE ACHTERGRACHT 17-23
AMSTERDAM

TELEPHONE 52915-52916.   TELEGR. ADDRESS: SOEPMUZ.

BENNO SOEP, INA'S BROTHER IN THE UNIFORM OF THE DUTCH ARMY
DRAFTEE WITH HIS SISTERS, JOSETTE, LEFT, AND INA, 1940.

JAAP POLAK WITH HIS FIRST WIFE, MANJA, AT THE TIME OF THEIR ENGAGE- MENT, 1939.

INA SOEP, 1942

Monday, February 7, 1944

Dear Sweetheart,

Just a few words in great haste. I can't tell you how happy I am that you got out of transport! But my joy is completely dulled by the fact that my mother-in-law is on the transport, and that in all probability, there is nothing to be done for her. Tomorrow, more. You can understand how Manja feels, although my mother-in-law is extremely strong. Tomorrow morning: Transport Service. There, I will have a very difficult time.

Till tomorrow,

Many, many kisses,

Jaap

Ina:

My trust in my father's connections was completely justified again. I always had faith that we would remain in Westerbork another week and another week, etc. But it was a very narrow escape for me, because the Germans did empty the entire hospital for deportation to Auschwitz. I was sent to a much smaller barrack, more like a little hall with ten or twelve women where I remained for a few more weeks, recuperating.

Being in such close contact with women only, we came, naturally, to talk about other physical conditions peculiar to women only, like menstruation. It was pretty generally known that women didn't menstruate in the camps. Thank God, they didn't! In my particular case, when I was cloistered in the Jewish Theater for five weeks, nothing happened. For ten weeks, when we were freed, I was normal. As soon as we arrived in Westerbork, and from then on for nineteen months thereafter, nothing. The day we rode into Holland in May after liberation, it happened. It's uncanny. Some people said that the Germans put something in the food, but that was too far-fetched. Maybe it has to do with nerves or apprehension, or maybe it's just nature's way of protecting us. I don't know.

———— ■ ■ ————

Tuesday, February 8, 1944

Dear Ineke,

It is now 11:00 A.M., and after this unnerving transport, I am sitting again in my office to start writing to you. It is really a miserable situation with my mother-in-law, because as I wrote yesterday, there was absolutely nothing to be done. She forfeited her rights to Theresienstadt, despite the fact that she had her "Palestine Certificate" added to ours in her bag. She was not granted any change in orders. She was very strong, and so were Manja and her sister. I must tell you very frankly that it was as bad for me as when other loved ones of mine went. You know that I loved my mother-in-law as a mother, and thus had the same feelings as when I had to say goodbye to my parents. In addition to this, one of my mother's sisters and her husband left on this lousy transport.

Now I haven't spoken at all about my joy that you got out of going. To tell you the truth, I had a feeling from the beginning that you had a good chance, especially since your father went to the "highest" sources. When I saw you yesterday morning to congratulate you and myself, I still didn't know anything about my mother-in-law. After visiting you, I went to my sister-in-law's who gave me the bad news. First I went to pick up Manja at the Industry, had a quick bite, had an errand to run, coming and going, packing, etc. Then I went straight to bed although I can't say I slept at all, and got up at 5:00 A.M. for Transport Duty. For this duty, I had to stand Special Watch between "49" and "50", where everybody passed, and I was able to talk to them. When my mother-in-law came, I was able to accompany her to the cattle car, where I found a small space for her. This is a short version of something that I could write many pages about. Of course I am dead tired, but I am already past being sleepy.

I now have to get my Special Certificate in order, and then to Celle. I must admit, it is slowly beginning to get to me here, mostly because you never know what to expect from one day to the next. Maybe it will be the same in Celle, but that's a gamble we'll have to take. Passenger trains on a transport give an entirely different impression than cattle cars, giving one special hopes. Hopefully, I will see you soon back in the barrack in good health. Many, many kisses and an extra one because of your "survival" from this transport.

My love as always

    Jaap

———■ ■———

Tuesday, February 8, 1944, 6:00 P.M.

My dear Ineke,

In between eating my spoonful of *stampot*–a little talk with you.

Every once in a while I have special thoughts which I would so love to tell you, but my head isn't really all together, as this afternoon we had to work hard to get the school back to normal again. Tomorrow morning we are having a Chamisha-Asar party; and if your Jewish brain doesn't know what that means, hon, it is really no disgrace. It is the New Year's Festival of the Trees in Israel. We will sing some songs with the children, some people will speak, and some will play music. How much I like this kind of thing you well know, but life goes on. I gave my mother-in-law two letters for my father and mother. Maybe they will get them.

Manja starts working tomorrow in Zichten, this week from 1:45 till 8:45 in the evening. Difficult work, and very unpleasant. Tonight, we will eat with my sister-in-law, and in all probability, I will stay there through the evening.

But my darling, please get out fast.

Would you like something to read? I just got some Dutch books which are worth reading.

I hope to come tomorrow afternoon, if my extremely busy work schedule doesn't prevent it as was the case this afternoon!

So, till then. Much, much love.

Jaap

———■ ■———

* *Stampot is a Dutch dish which consists of a vegetable like spinach or kale mashed together with potatoes.*

Wednesday evening, February 9, 1944, 10:15 P.M.
My dearest Ineke,

I really had planned to write to you at 6:00 P.M., but then I had to get some food for Manja at my aunt's, so nothing came of it. Even tonight, I couldn't do anything as I had to clean up until 9:00 P.M., and I'm not even half finished. Then I received a number of things from "49", after which my bed looked like a baggage bed for twenty people. Tomorrow evening, I will continue while Manja will do laundry, repair, straighten up, etc. So we are really getting ready for the transport, which is slowly becoming a reality. I'll tell you honestly that if they try to get us out of the transport through either the School or Industry connections, we will not take the risk. Because of what happened with the last transport, it seems much safer to go to Celle with our "Palestine Papers" in our pockets. As to you, I give you my opinion about this transport right here. Of course, it is a little difficult to have to go to Celle with "Palestine Papers" or "120,000 Certificates." But I still advise you for more than one reason, that if you are healthy enough to go on this transport, you should go. It would be really crazy and great if we could stay together in this way. The crazy thing is that when things were totally right between us, a departure together, or a joint destination looked almost impossible. Now, when we are separated, we are either going to be sent together, or at least have a joint destination. I do anticipate, with my always present optimistic feelings, (if nothing happens), we will both end up together in Celle.

Sweet darling, the lights are going out, so for tonight that's all. Tomorrow morning, more on the typewriter.

Many, many goodnight kisses,
Jaap

In great haste, a few more words. There is still a small possibility that we aren't going Tuesday. This is completely contrary to Wednesday night's letter. That's Westerbork!!!

Ina:

One of the big luxuries in Westerbork was to have an unoccupied bed near you with no mattress on it, just the bunk with metal strips, because you could get rid of your belongings. If the bed was occupied, everything had to go underneath the bunkbed, and it was damp there, and hard to get to–dirty and dusty. So when there was a baggage bed nearby, an empty bed where you could store your things, it was quite a luxury. Till this day, whenever we go anywhere and I can put my pocketbook on a chair or a stool instead of on the floor, I always say, "There's a baggage bed!"

———■ ■———

Thursday evening, February 10, 1944, 7:30 P.M.

Dearest Ineke,

As you could probably tell from the look on my face this afternoon, I am dead tired, due to a combination of complicated work and business problems. First of all at school, where it is so busy that I am quickly going crazy, everybody, even the school children, come to me for everything, no doubt a great honor; but I told them today that they must think about what they will do next week when I'm not there, that then they must go to someone else.

In the meantime, I found out that Rabbi Frank is doing his best to put me on the "1,000 list." Not that I have a great desire to be on it, but on the other hand, all the Amsterdammers tell me that it gets more important every week in view of what they feel is the coming invasion. (I have to see that first, then I will do something about it.) There is also the fact that we have to move tomorrow. We're going to Barrack 69, and are very lucky because we know the Barrack

Leader and the Ward Leaders; so I have been given the top bunk bed and a table!! Manja also got the last top bunk. For how long?

Now about you. I was very happy that you felt somewhat better today than yesterday. Hopefully, the jaundice will disappear. You've surely had more than your share.

I would like to have been housed with your parents, but I didn't have a good feeling about Barrack 63, for the same reason that you didn't like it. But don't feel uneasy about our correspondence. That will be taken care of. Potentially, you can give your letters to Selma, who will give them to me via Frouk. She has known about us for a long time!

The days fly by now because of the busy work schedule. I also really miss the nice evenings we used to have. Do you still remember? My sister-in-law and Manja have not yet gotten over my mother-in-law's departure. And that she had to leave on a transport is really quite bad; but we are really convinced that she will pull through barring unforeseen difficulties.

Now a few words about your coming departure. It makes sense to combine ours together, but I can't advise you as to what to do. I think that I'll just let things take their own course. If they really want to keep me here, and it works out well, fine. If not, then we leave. I really do feel that we will see each other in Celle. Sweet darling, the paper is full. Maybe more tonight in bed.

Many, many kisses,

Jaap

———■　■———

Friday afternoon, February 11, 1944, 4:30 P.M.

Dearest girl,

Just a few words while I'm getting a haircut, something badly needed for many weeks. I used the excuse that I was moving! It was really very tough, but fortunately, we "made it." It was much easier for you to move from "64" to "63," hardly a step! There hasn't been any change in our situation as of yet. People are saying that the camp will become an Industry Camp, and it will be possible for us to stay here with special Industry Saving Papers. We would have the ability to retain our Celle rights, which wouldn't be too bad; because, in any event, after this transport, there will be more transports to Celle. Furthermore, it is always possible to ask for a Theresienstadt-Visa, as I wrote you yesterday, I think. Sweet darling, this is not my "official" letter, but just a little scribble for today. Tonight, more.

For the moment, many, many kisses,

Jaap

———■　■———

Friday evening, February 11, 1944, 5:45 P.M.

Dear Ineke,

As I finally got a break from *davening next door, I can now talk with you for a while. About the Celle transport: although we're getting everything ready, I feel that my chances of going are fifty-fifty. And it is probably the same with you. As long as you are in the same fifty as I, it will be good. Additionally, I believe that the decision will be made at the last moment, probably not until Sunday or Monday.

I was really lucky to get the highest bunk and a table in the "69" Barrack, but I don't know what I'm going to do with all my junk. For a few days, it really doesn't matter; and if it is longer, there will be more room after Tuesday's transport.

Now there is a rumor that there won't be a transport to Celle, only one to Theresienstadt, but I don't believe that IPA. My dear Ineke, this is about all the news. This may be, but I hope not, my goodbye letter. See you soon, or better said, "write you soon". All the best with your health.

Much, much love,

Jaap

P.S. How are you sleeping these days? What does your father say that you should do on Tuesday? Does Josette have to go anyway? Now you have to write to me again.

*Davening refers to the Orthodox Jewish ritual of praying.

———■　■———

91

Saturday afternoon, February 12, 1944, at school, 3:45 P.M.
Sweet Darling,

First of all, this morning we received our notice that we will be transported to another camp, a semi-official call. So we immediately started to pack. Still, our chances are always fifty-fifty, and if Theresienstadt were to be called off, it would be best for both of us!! The most important thing is that Rabbi Frank, in my case, and the Industry, in Manja's, (the latter being much more important than the former!), will get us out of this transport, until the next Celle transport, which the IPA's say will take place in 5 weeks! Our Sperre papers would not be taken away in this case, although we do run risks in this way of becoming victims. They say that for the moment, there will be no more Auschwitz transports; and that there will be a real Industrial Camp, where work merits will be rewarded with slips of paper which can be used in exchange for articles in the canteen. It's all too wonderful for words.

In any event, if I go, or if you go, you will get a longer letter from me.

I am very anxious to know what you are going to do, and it is impossible for me to give you guidance. A lot depends on how you feel! The *BDS* and the "120,000 Diamond List" haven't been called yet, but it may happen tomorrow.

I am now going to my sister-in-law's (although I might surprise someone first?!). The route of our letters is safe, and the only problem is that I don't know how to seal them, but that really doesn't matter.

Kisses and much, much love,
Jaap

BDS refers to people with dual citizenship such as British and Dutch.

Jaap:

We had more things in Westerbork than we needed, because we thought we were going to a labor camp. For example, I had 2 suits, a bottle of cologne, duplicates of shoes, (we were issued wooden shoes for muddy, outdoor work), so many things were completely extraneous and burdensome.

———■　■———

Sunday afternoon, February 13, 1944, 2:15 P.M.

Dearest Ineke,

The situation is still the same as yesterday, and I assume that I won't know before Monday afternoon whether I will go on transport or not. And it is not known how it is with you either at this moment while I write, as the list has not come through yet, though it could arrive any minute.

Tomorrow morning I have "early service." I have to bring our laundry at 6:00 A.M. to the laundry room, so that everything will be clean before the transport. Will you think of me?

Last night was quiet. I was able to read at my sister-in-law's while the ladies made their transport preparations.

Till tomorrow. I hope that I can say the same thing on Wednesday.

Much, much love,

Jaap

P.S. Hurrah for your "Palestine Papers!" If I don't go tomorrow, I can see the possibility of us departing together.

———■　■———

Monday evening, February 14, 1944, 10:30 P.M.
My dearest lady,

It is now the evening before my departure, which despite everything still came fairly unexpectedly. All I want to say is that my departure from here makes me very sad and that is only for one reason. But I hope that you will soon follow me, even if the dual nature of our relationship would start again in all its aspects. I know darned well that there is a good possibility that after the war, or after a longer period, if I get a divorce, I may have lost you because of this dual nature. But maybe everything will go without a hitch, like in the first months here when everything went quietly and peacefully. I cannot tell you how terrible I feel to leave you in this way. But nothing can be done.

Sweet darling, if you spend the war here, you can always go to my good friend, Simon Stork, for information. He will know where to reach me. Especially because Liesje is leaving with us, everything will be done to get us back. It is great that you are staying together with Josette, great for all of you.

I already said goodbye to your father and Josette. I didn't see your mother, but asked your papa to give her my regards.

Dearest Ineke, this is not just a departure letter. Only a wish for a very, very speedy coming together for us.

Embraces and love,

Jaap

———■ ■———

BERGEN-BELSEN CONCENTRATION CAMP

Bergen and Belsen were two small villages located about 25 kilometers north of Celle, a town in northwestern Germany. The camp there had been established as a prisoner-of-war camp, but was changed from that designation in July 1943, to become a Nazi concentration camp intended for the Jews whom the German government wished to exchange for German nationals held in Allied territory. In April 1943, the head of the SS, Himmler, ordered the transport of 10,000 so-called "exchange Jews" into this central camp. Its inmates were Jews possessing passports or citizenship papers of Latin American states, entry visas for Palestine, hostages, prisoners who had paid a ransom, and others. Only two prisoner exchanges ever took place: 136 inmates were sent to Switzerland, and 222 to Palestine.

Initially, the camp inmates who were to be exchanged escaped most of the brutalities which were common practice in concentration camps, so they would never be in a position to report on SS cruelties. But gradually, the detention camp Bergen-Belsen came into existence; and it began to receive other prisoners who were divided

95

from one another into various camp sections. These inmates were strictly separated, and endured varying living conditions according to their status as decreed by the SS.

The camp site was able to quarter 10,000 inmates, and conditions, although difficult, were at first better than in other camps. But during 1944, there was a change for the worse. Food rations were reduced to below minimum requirements, and prisoners were cruelly beaten, and forced to do hard labor. In addition, whether from malicious intent, or for lack of administrative facilities, the camp authorities failed to provide even minimal essential services.

When most of the prisoners had reached the point of physical and mental collapse, they were joined by prisoners who had been removed from other concentration camps near the front lines as a result of the German retreat. The situation became catastrophic. The Bergen-Belsen population swelled rapidly from 15,000 in December 1944, to 41,000 by March 1945. During those last weeks, there was an additional massive influx of prisoners from the East. These new prisoners arrived after forced marches sometimes lasting weeks, and were starved and disease-ridden. Epidemics broke out, but there was no medical attention to be had. The camp authorities deliberately refrained from easing the situation, and made no attempt to draw on the reserves of food, clothing, and medical supplies stored at nearby military camps. The death rate was enormously high, and rose to nearly 20,000 people dead during the month of March 1945, (including Anne Frank). A total of 37,000 died before the liberation.

Bergen-Belsen was the first camp to be liberated by the British Army on April 15, 1945. By that time, it was a camp sinking under the weight of the human misery the Germans had created. The horrors which deeply shocked the British soldiers received widespread publicity in the West. The British arrested the SS administrators, and almost all were put to work burying the thousands of corpses. Those who did not die doing this work were tried by the Allies at the end of 1945.

ARRIVAL IN BERGEN-BELSEN

JAAP POLAK

Jaap:

From Westerbork 103,000 Jews were deported: 93,000 went directly to the extermination camps; 10,000 were the "lucky" ones who were sent only to concentration camps. I belonged to the "lucky" ones to be sent to Bergen-Belsen.

On Tuesday morning, February 15, 1944, I left Westerbork together with 773 people. All we knew was that we were being sent to a "privileged camp", as stated on our travel orders because of our Palestine papers. Compared to leaving on the other transports, we felt a little better because we were on a regular train, not a cattle car, but still extremely nervous, as nobody knew what to expect at the other end. We had packed as much as we could in our rucksacks, clothing as well as food. We did not realize how smart this was to do, until we found out later how many of the things we could use for bartering. The actual departure was harrowing. I watched the German Commandant inspecting his "troops", the German-Jews in charge, the "big shots" in the camp, and thought, "How can we ever convey to the rest of the world what is happening here?"

And still when I thought about the experiences of the previous months in Westerbork when so many times I was part of the group of people put in charge of placing the sick, infants-in-arms, the old, even my own father and mother, and so many of my friends and other relatives in cattle cars, sixty to eighty people to a car, I realized that I MIGHT have a chance to survive. I never could have guessed then how lucky I was going to be.

I recall our arrival at Bergen-Belsen. Our luggage was put on trucks, though we were reluctant to part with it, not sure if we would ever see it again. Then we walked for about two hours and arrived at the camp where we immediately sensed a dismal, foreboding atmosphere. We could keep our clothing, our luggage and our hair, but I remember seeing Ina's sister-in-law through the barbed wire, and all she signaled to me was her bent finger, which was enough for me to know that we should not raise our expectations for anything too good.

————■　■————

February, 1944

Jaap:

Once in a while, the Germans permitted you to write a postcard, so shortly after I arrived I wrote to Ina. It was very strictly stipulated that it must be written in German only, with thirty to thirty-five words allowed. The following is what I wrote:

Catharina Soep
Born 1/3/1923
Lager: WESTERBORK   Jaap Polak
Hooghalen, W. HOLLAND   BERGEN-BELSEN
    Dearest Ineke,

I am very healthy and in good spirits. I feel this great longing for you. Tell friends to send packages; also to Liesje and Manja. Received your letter. I hope to see you very, very soon. Regards to all. Many kisses, your Jaap

Ina:

The postcard arrived in Westerbork months later, after I had already reached Bergen-Belsen; but my parents had remained there because my mother was ill with hepatitis. So my parents received the postcard meant for me, having no knowledge at all about my relationship. They were shocked and quite surprised—not pleasantly either!

———■ ■———

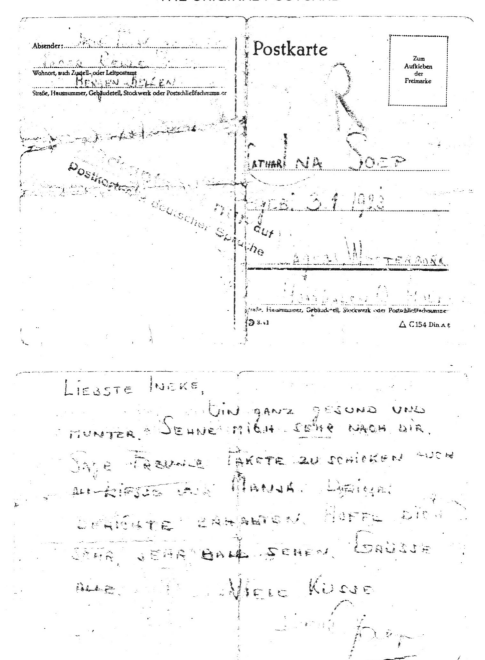

Tuesday evening, February 29, 1944

My dearest Ineke,

Before your hoped for arrival, I want to tell you that a major part of my time has been filled with thoughts about you. Not only about you, but also about my own future. When I think idealistically about this future, you are always in my thoughts, by my side. I do have some well grounded hopes that our being together here in Celle, both possessing Palestine Certificates, will enable us to come out together after the war, and in that way we can decide about our future together.

We have a "soft" life here in quarantine, because since the day of our arrival we have all been confined. My daily program consists of getting up in the morning around 6:15 A.M., (every other day a shave); 7:00 A.M., some food with drinkable coffee; from 7:30 to 9:00, I help the cleaning staff clean the barrack; from 9:00–10:00, I occupy myself in the barrack with small things such as shining my shoes; from 10:00 till around 11:00, a roll call outside, then 11 to 12:30 P.M., bridge, little card games, chess, reading or studying; 12:30 P.M.–1:30 P.M., a meal; from 1:30 to 5:00 P.M., the same as the morning routine; 5:00 P.M., a meal, 6:00 P.M. to 7:00, a visit to the ladies' barracks, (which I sometimes do during the day, but not that often); 7:00 P.M.–8:00 P.M., bridge. At 8:00 P.M., I go to bed and sleep well, despite the fact that I get up at least three times a night, because I drink so much during the day, for all they give you here is soup.

For the people who work it is very, very hard; and that is the reason that I hope you too will go into quarantine. Also, the sleeping arrangement in the barrack is much more crowded than in Westerbork, and that won't be any good for your asthma. Hopefully, you are now in perfect health, and will be well able to withstand the circumstances here.

Food here is good, but if you go to work-not enough, so be very stingy with the food which I hope you take along. As you see from my daily program, I have a good life here so far. We have a very cozy barrack with many people I know well. There is a good cultural life here. We speak Hebrew two or three times a week, have Zionist meetings three times a week, and I even enjoy the Sabbath celebration. Manja and Liesje are in the same barrack, which is why I talk to Liesje and the children regularly. Juul is lucky to be a teacher, although we aren't officially allowed to have a school. Freddy has a very difficult job as a fire stoker, and carrying the sick to the hospital. Liesje also has a very tough job as a nurse in the hospital. Because of the quarantine, I don't see them too much, but I do have some contact with the outside world, as I am carrying food barrels. When someone meets me at the gate and takes over, I have a chance to talk to them.

Lady of mine, I am very anxious to hear from you, also all the Westerbork news.

Many, many kisses, and we have to catch up for what we missed on paper in the last two weeks.

Jaap

P.S. My barrack number is 10C.

———■   ■———

Jaap:

Being in quarantine was like being in a holding place. The Germans didn't know what they were going to do with us. They knew we were "privileged" people in some way, either diamond people, or Palestine people, or of foreign nationality. They knew we were not doomed yet, and they had no reason to start killing us. What should they do with us? Should we work, should we not work, what kind of work should we be given? Everyone was put in quarantine for about two weeks to see if anybody would get sick, and they could then keep illnesses from spreading through the camp.

I was in a section of the camp that would eventually house Ina and her family too, called Sternlager, or Star Camp. Only the privileged "exchange Jews" were imprisoned here. Sternlager meant that inmates were permitted to wear civilian clothes with the yellow star of David. Bergen-Belsen was a work camp; so work was obligatory, even for old people. Men and women were accommodated separately, but families could meet during the day.

Our treatment in the beginning was better, our food a little more substantial, and our work life somewhat easier than that of other sections of the camp; although later, the same horrible conditions prevailed throughout the camp for all prisoners.

——■　■——

Tuesday night, March 7, 1944

My dear little lady,

Again a week has passed, and given the preparations here, I believe that at this moment you are in a train headed this way.

A new camp like Celle gives you so many impressions, each day, with so many Jews having so many problems, that ten times a day I have the feeling that I want to tell you things so badly. But it is almost impossible to sit and write because there's no time, which sounds crazy from someone who in reality has nothing to do, but my free time has slowly been diminished; because I have become administrator of my barrack, a job which mainly consists of making lists and keeping track of everybody's food. Furthermore, I work in the cleaning service for the barrack; and finally, I have to haul the food barrels, which is really the heaviest part of my work. But I feel good and healthy, and I have even acquired a tan from the sun.

In my last letter, I spoke about dreams for the future, and maybe it is crazy that these dreams seem like much more of a reality here than in Westerbork. This is probably because the circumstances here are so much more difficult, especially with regard to food. And then you start thinking about how glad you will be later with an ordinary breakfast, a good bed, an ordinary shower or bath, not to mention all the other pleasures in life like going out, etc... I think that in my future life, if I make it, I will be able to value even the smallest things, things that I didn't understand the value of before. Which brings me back to my first letter, where I said it is not my intention to go through life alone, and with Manja it will _never_ work; I have discussed this again with her, and we both agree completely on this. When you consider the harmony and the similarity in feelings which we had on so many matters which we discussed in those beautiful first months in Westerbork when we got to know each other, I do believe that we could, in a normal world, have a good life together. But despite this, I believe it will still be necessary to get to know each other again in a normal world.

I hope to get a big letter from you, assuming that we won't be able to see each other due to your quarantine. Please let me know:

a. How you are <u>and</u>, were you still in the hospital until the end?

b. How your parents are and how is the "Diamond List?" (Are they coming here too, will there be another transport, or is yours the last one?)

c. What transports left after our Celle transport went out and which people do we know that went with them; and what is the consensus about the future of the camp, Barneveld, Barrack 73, and the "1,000 list?"

d. Political news.

I work quite regularly on English grammar, and English economics, and Hebrew. Furthermore, I have two English detective stories and one novel to read, "Castle in Corinth" by Fabricius.

It is now 8:15 P.M., which is very late by Celle standards, so I'm going to turn in.

My dear little lady, you are arriving here on *Purim*. Let us hope, in any event, to celebrate Purim next year in freedom, if possible together, and if God will grant us this for our destiny, in our own home and family circle.

Try to be strong here, it won't be easy; but spirits up, we <u>*must*</u> *survive*.

Kisses and love,

Jaap

Purim is the Jewish carnival-like festival, celebrating the events of "The Book of Esther". This tells of Haman's plot to destroy the Jews of Persia, and Queen Esther and her uncle Mordechai's successful efforts, through intervention with the King, to save their people.

——— ■   ■ ———

Tuesday evening, March 14, 1944, 7:30 P.M.

Sweet darling,

Just a few words by flashlight (there is an air raid alarm and no lights on). I am now in Barrack 11H. I am doing nasty work, digging under the supervision of the SS from 6 in the morning until 6 in the evening. I am dead tired but in good health, though that won't last long.

Many, many kisses,
Jaap

———■　■———

Jaap:

After a few weeks I was assigned to the so called "Stubben Kommando," the most infamous of all work commandos, whose task was the clearing of woodlands. It was the hardest labor, performed in any kind of weather. We were guarded by the brutal SS men with their German shepherds constantly surrounding us. I did not think that I could last too long. I would say it was the worst experience of my life digging up the ground, and hacking on trees—never able to slow down or rest. I don't think that anybody working in those outside commandos survived. It was horrible.

Fortunately for me, when I heard that they were looking for kitchen workers, I showed up for roll-call, and they asked for experienced people for the kitchen. I told them I had worked at the Carlton Hotel, a very fine hotel in Amsterdam. Although I had only been an administrator there, they took it for granted that I had done kitchen work. It was grueling work, and it meant getting up in the middle of the night at 3:00 A.M. to begin work. But I was motivated by the fact that I could get more food to eat there, and I could try to steal some food as well to bring into the barrack for other people.

There were two kitchens. We prepared food under the direction of SS men. The Number One kitchen prepared food for the Germans. First, the entire kitchen had to be cleaned, then coffee was made for the entire camp. We put the coffee in huge cans for distribution to the rest of the camp. I did a lot of potato peeling, and I spent most of the day stirring boiling kettles of soup.

I lasted for about two weeks in the kitchen until I was thrown out; because we had to lift heavy bags of sugar, and not knowing how to handle these heavy bags, I toppled over with one. Soon after that incident, I was transferred to work in the shoe factory.

I was put to work in a separate barrack, seated at a very long table with about 100 other men, taking apart old shoes. It was obvious to us that the Germans intended to use the leather, laces, soles, etc. separately for industrial purposes.

We had no indicator or notion that these were the shoes taken from Jewish people in other camps, certainly not in extermination camps, as we had no knowledge of them. We just thought that these were old shoes, discarded by the German people to be recycled.

It was of course a dirty job, and the dust spread all over us and on everything near us. The odors were nauseating.

But as loathsome as the work was, we were able to make our days interesting by having debates and even lectures while we were working. We would listen to the lectures by people who had been prominent in their field in normal times, all under the suspicious eyes of the German guards. Most times the lectures were spoken in whispers.

———■ ■———

ARRIVAL IN BERGEN-BELSEN
INA SOEP

Ina:

We left Westerbork in passenger cars of the Dutch Railroad on May 18, 1944, for Bergen-Belsen. It was roughly a 24-hour trip until our arrival at the nearest station in Celle. A lot of soldiers in green uniforms, many holding German shepherds barking and straining at their leashes, were the first images we received. Once we were off the train, I spotted a man whom I recognized from Westerbork who later became the leader of the Jews in the division we were assigned to, and still later, became my uncle through marriage. I peppered him with questions about the camp, the work, the conditions, people I knew who had already arrived, etc. He was a very quiet, reserved person and tried to appease me with, "It is not too bad, we are managing." I can still see him moving his hands up and down in a soothing manner.

We had to surrender our luggage which was loaded on to trucks, and except for the very old and very young who were transported in trucks, we walked to camp which took about two hours. Our first sighting of the camp gave us the chilling impression of rows and rows of barbed wire and watch towers everywhere surrounding it. It was situated on a heath near Hanover on very flat, sandy grounds, with nothing to relieve the sight of endless barracks in a huge compound divided into many different sections. We didn't really know just how many different ones there were, for we were just brought to one place. Before being assigned to our permanent housing, we were immediately placed in a quarantine barrack for about a week, and then removed to the section called the Sternlager, or "Star Camp." We were permitted to wear our own clothing, which was a very distinct privilege.

My sister and I wound up in permanent quarters with all the people connected with the diamond industry, even though my parents were not with us. They had to stay back in Westerbork, because my mother was very ill with hepatitis. They didn't arrive until September 1944, four months later, with the last transport.

The group that my family was put together with were all involved in the diamond business: from the biggest tycoons to the lowliest cutters. The idea was to save the hands of the workers, and the expertise of the manufacturers, to satisfy the Germans' eventual goal of setting up a diamond industry in Bergen-Belsen. No one in this group was required to work. All we did all day was to try and keep warm and fed; and we stood for roll call by the hour. The women diamond cutters were really a special breed of people.

Their "esprit de corps" was truly earthy–very basic with a wonderful brand of humor. We laughed a lot with them. Every night, before we went to sleep, after the SS men yelled at the door, "Lichter aus !", "Lights out!", we would recite a rhyme in unison, which freely translated, says, "Notwithstanding the hard day and the difficult separation, still we are a day closer to our liberation." That was the kind of attitude people clung to as long as they could hold out, until they were so desperate from illness, or weakness, or hunger, that there was nothing more for them to look forward to. For myself, I felt it was unthinkable to imagine that I would die. I was young, with no responsibilities; and with the feelings of invincibility of the young which Jaap, with his dogged optimism, certainly fortified for me! We lived for ourselves from day to day, and we always believed we were going to survive.

———■   ■———

May 1944

Dear Ineke,

At last! It was great to be able to see you for a moment this afternoon, even though we couldn't talk quietly. As I told you then, it's not going to be very easy, but those moments will come again soon. Your presence here is already a ray of light for me. As it was in Westerbork, I feel completely at ease with you. How is that with you darling? Do you feel everything is the same as in the beginning in Westerbork; or has our relationship perhaps suffered due to the difficult last months there? Tell me very honestly if you have the same happy, peaceful, and loving feelings for me now as in our wonderful beginning. I am very anxious to know! If you answer me now, you will then get a long letter from me, that is if I am still working in the shoe department. You don't do much work here besides thinking, a healthy occupation, especially because in my case the subject of interest for me is not very faraway!

Enough for today,

Kisses and embraces (we have a whole lot to catch up on!)

your Jaap

———■   ■———

May 20, 1944

Ineke, my darling,

A few words for you in between the "shoes." Now that you are here, it is as if I have found peace of mind again. And as long as we use what Manja calls "common sense," I believe that, especially in the very difficult circumstances in which we live here, we will be able to be of support to each other. Do you know what I was thinking about in bed last night? (Among other things!) How crazy it really is that our departure, as well as our reunion both took place completely platonically. Maybe it was also better this way; but you mustn't think that because of that I am affected platonically. But I think that you think the same way! Manja said to me yesterday that she does not plan to be just my housekeeper; because I only go to her to pick up some food, or have something washed. I can understand that, but on the other hand, the most important thing for me is seeing you regularly, even if it is for a short while, but at least *openly*. And we can do that now. So darling, in this way we begin our newest stage, hopefully lasting until the end of the war, and then maybe we can have a new beginning. If only we were that far already! In my thoughts, and I am afraid that here in Celle it will have to stay that way! I kiss you,

your Jaap

P.S. Excuse my extremely bad handwriting; but writing here at this table made of rough stone is far from easy.

—————■   ■—————

Tuesday, May 23, 1944

Dearest Ineke:

Just a quiet moment to talk with you. That is at least one advantage I have over you here, the ability to concentrate on my thoughts. But if everything is O.K. in Barrack 17, then a non-working life is just beginning for you, and it will also be easy for you to find moments of quiet concentration.

For the moment, I am glad enough just to be a very close friend of yours. It is impossible to have an actual relationship here anyway. On the one hand, that is quite a pity, assuming that you long for me as much as I do for you; but everything here is completely different than in Westerbork, and you will find that a love life, for man and wife as well as for a young couple, is completely nonexistent. But on the other hand, with the knowledge that I am just a "real companion" of yours, I will not have to accept any more blame from Manja. I have also made my position here much clearer than in Westerbork (my greatest mistake there!), and all this gives me a certain feeling of freedom and ease when I speak with you. But I mustn't overdo it, as long as we, or maybe you more than I, don't feel safe about our relationship. The saddest part, of course, is that we have to miss the wonderful, peaceful talks that we used to have on our many walks in those first months in Westerbork, (even our talks in silence were good!). So for us, it is sufficient to know that we are close to each other, and have a good chance of staying here together until the end of the war, an advantage over thousands of other Jews. You know what I always say about Our Good Lord. Maybe it really is the truth!

Finally, just one more thing. You are afraid, that in the end, you will be in second place behind Manja. You shouldn't have this fear. You were always "No. 1" to me.

Enough for today. I believe that I will only have a truly clear mind after I have left this *beautiful place*. Here, it is as if you slowly wither away; and because of that, the feeling of your presence is such a joy.

Good night sweetheart, assuming that you read this letter before you go to sleep. Sleep well, and have good dreams about someone who loves you very much and kisses you,

Jaap

Ina:

At first, it seemed strange to me that Jaap placed so much emphasis on the importance of our "talks" that we had in the first months in Westerbork. But as time wore on in the camp here, I gradually began to understand how we had truly laid the foundation for everything that is recommended for young couples to explore before taking marriage vows. As it became more and more exasperating for us to find opportunities to even meet–much less, talk–those "talks" did take on their rightful importance. Solid exchanges of ideas and feelings about what we expected of life, and of a life-time partner, indicated that we had, miraculously, found what each of us was looking for.

———■   ■———

Wednesday, May 24, 1944

My Ineke:

It was great to see you for a moment this afternoon, even if it was short, and I intend to see you every day either on my way back to work, or when you come and see me later. This way I have better things to think about than food, which is the main topic of discussion the whole morning.

I will not accept objections from Manja, as I hardly see you at all in the evening.

My letters from now on will probably bear my work stamp on them: words on dirty, wrinkled paper. But you must take it as it is! In the name of love.

I really like your idea for us to exchange our letters. As soon as I am finished sorting them, you will get yours. Please give me mine as soon as possible.

And one more thing before I forget it. Here in this camp, we find big surprises everyday, and it is thus quite possible that we might suddenly be separated again, without a chance to say goodbye, or to make plans. Let us talk over an arrangement for what we would do then, hopefully more concretely than in Westerbork. Didn't you also make arrangements with your parents in case you don't meet them here?

Darling, this letter is really nothing special. A real everyday garden-variety conversation written with a pencil without a point. Sleep well; kisses from your Jaap.

———■ ■———

Ina:

I suggested the exchange of letters so that each of us could carry our own writings with us, because I felt so uncertain about what the future would bring; and the longer we were in the camp with worsening conditions every day, the more uncertain I felt. Would we be separated and never see each other again? Would either one of us or both survive? At least this way, each of us could decide at any given moment what to do with our own letters containing our own experiences, thoughts and feelings. I did not want my privacy violated by curious eyes reading my letters, and I knew Jaap would feel the same way.

Thursday, May 25, 1944

My sweet darling,

The first thing we talked about here today was food, then I slept for half an hour, of course with some risk, but it was still nice; and after that, for appearance's sake, I cut a few shoes. It was great to finally be with you in peace this afternoon, and I hope that you enjoyed it as well, even though we didn't have too much to say at the time.

Now something else. When I think about the future, I of course envision launching a happy marriage under normal circumstances. But for that, it is necessary to stay fit both mentally and physically. When you look at how some people degenerate in both ways here, I become terrified in my heart. If I, therefore, try in every way to get as much food as possible, you must not think that I am in the habit of doing things like this, but only that I have the will to get my body to its maximum strength; especially since we do not know how long it's

117

all going to take, and what we will still have to go through. And as to mental fitness, I do want to keep learning, doing Hebrew and English, and not talking only about the IPA's and food. Fortunately, there are enough of this kind of men here in the shoe factory, so that every once in a while we can wander off to the W.C., and talk for fifteen minutes about different things. And I also feel mentally uplifted when I am together with you, even when we sit together and don't say a word. For you, these problems are not as pressing as for me here, where long working hours and deadly, boring work create these problems. But still you must prepare yourself by keeping fit, and we will hopefully come through this together in not too long a period of time, and in not too bad shape. So Ineke, this is enough, and I stop. Everyone wants me to write in my notes that we are all very hungry. They think I'm keeping a diary.

Till tomorrow,

Kisses,

Your Jaap

Ina:

We were hungry all the time. We got a piece of bread in the morning which we sliced as thin as possible so we could feel that it was more than it was, and that had to last for the whole day, with a little pat of margarine. For breakfast, we had that and imitation coffee, which was brought into the barracks in huge, heavy mess tins. The coffee was made of chicory and it was very sweet, but at least it looked like coffee. Lunch was a watery soup with turnips, and there was sometimes a little horsemeat or potato in it. There were always fights because the person ladling out the soup would sometimes give more meat or potatoes to somebody. It was awful. I remember often sitting on the bed, with my feet

118

around the warm bowl, or my hands around my mug with the coffee. Dinner was just bread and coffee again, although sometimes we would get more soup.

Like most of the members of the diamond group, I did not work in the beginning of my stay in Bergen-Belsen, because the Germans wanted our hands to be saved for work in the diamond factory that they still planned to establish in the camp.

——— ■ ■ ———

Sunday morning, May 28, 1944

My dearest Ineke,

Isn't the weather beautiful? Try to take advantage of it. I hope to do the same this afternoon. Last night, Manja and I again discussed our relationship. As sensible people, and you know I am referring to Manja's "sensible" claim, which we must take into consideration, you and I might have to see somewhat less of each other in the near future. Last night, Manja of course saw us taking a walk, but she made only one sarcastic remark, "Nice weather for a walk." You know that I put my foot down about seeing you regularly; so I take it for granted that she has agreed, because she acted normally, despite the knowledge of our walk. And do know that for me there remains only one "No. 1." Do you believe me, Ineke? I really hope so, because it would be a shame if the only nice thing that Celle has to offer would be ruined by things such as these.

This was my Sunday morning talk and so now, for my own sake, I go back to cutting up shoes.

See you later,
Many, many kisses
your Jaap

Monday May 29, 1944

My sweet darling,

It is now 12:00, and with hungry stomach I am waiting for the end of the air raid alarm. And although I have to keep working, I cant think of anything better to do than what we usually do at this time, namely to talk a bit withy you. My day tomorrow starts at around 6:45, when I'll be just to the left of Barrack 17, so look for me; although I don't want you to get up early just for me; but I don't think that will be the case, as due to the warm weather everyone is chased out of their beds early by the noise and stuffiness. On the one hand, an air raid at this hour is bad luck, but on the other hand, we would see each other , which since we hardly get to do that at in this camp, I hope is the case. Tonight we will have a few minutes together after my evening soup, which I must eat first. But then we will go to bed later, and tell you the truth, it is important with this warm weather that we try to go to bed early..

My dear girl, I am really just chattering on about nothing, but I also don't have that much to tell you.

More later, when we meet at roll call squares, or sitting on my bed.

Till later, I kiss you in my thoughts,
by your Jaap

Ina:

Our problems were always caused by Manja, who behaved mercurially, first allowing, then forbidding us to see each other, depending on her moods or her own circumstances of the moment. We could understand her discomfort vis-a-vis other people and their judgments. However in Bergen-Belsen, interestingly, there were many instances of couples being seen with people other than their spouses. In those circumstances, people were looking for some happiness and pleasure, and kind of ignoring what others might say about it. It was as if appearances were of little consequence anywhere–the barriers were down–the guardedness down; and it gave others the pleasure and diversion of gossip! Several of those "switched couples" married after the war, sometimes facilitated by the death of one of the spouses.

———■ ■———

Wednesday, May 31, 1944

My dearest little lady,

Some days are bad here: for instance, today.

Early this morning, I had food-kettle service, after which I lost my job; then a bad meal, and finally, the most important thing, as we both know, although we didn't think it would happen again after such a short period, is now the case again. At 12:30 P.M., I had a long talk with Manja. This morning two parties informed her where and when we are meeting each other. I could really kill these stupid and tactless women, in fact her too.

However, this time there are really a lot of differences.

1. I am much more self-assured in my feelings for you.

2. My feelings about Manja are definitely more negative, (please understand me); and in addition, Manja and I talked everything over in a better way.

The choice that Manja gave me is in fact the same: either limit my contact with you to only greeting you, or maybe exchanging a few words, or sever all contact with her. In other words, she doesn't want to see me any more. The choice is much more difficult for me here than in Westerbork; because there I knew that under the circumstances, I could not reasonably break off with her. Here, the situation is completely different.

First of all, I am much more positively inclined towards you, and I truly believe that I love you and can be happy with you in the future. Secondly, I think about all the problems that I caused you before, and I would not like this to happen for a second time.

There are a few other sides to this matter:

First of all, if you state your definite feelings, it would at least make things clear. In fact you will have to, because we have completely different circumstances to consider here than in Westerbork. If we are seen together here in the future, without anyone seeing me with Manja anymore, it will be accepted as an official relationship. I must draw your attention to something, and that is your reputation. Manja referred to this, and even I see it that way; for in Celle, it is much worse than in Westerbork. If we are together *officially* here, then it can only be with the statement that "later we are going to get married." And here I come to a proposal for a compromise: That is, that this is such a difficult matter, and you are so young, that I think, assuming that you want to stick with me, we may need to have another personal discussion. First of all, you have to decide if you dare to. Secondly, do you think that it might be wiser to wait until your father is here, and then I or we can talk everything over with him? I am talking here about the old-fashioned feelings about the happiness of their children being very close to the hearts of their parents. I think it would be very bad for us both, and even more so for you, if, when your parents come here, their daughter is involved in a scandal. As happy as we are together, people will still look at it in that way.

That would in fact mean that until the next Westerbork transport, we would barely see each other. You probably think that this is exactly the same situation as in Westerbork. I tell you in total honesty, that that is not the case.

Believe me, as friendly as Manja is to me again, Ineke, I do not fall for it: and an even stronger reason is that I will not forgive her for making things so difficult for the second time. And even if I do see her, then despite the appearance of something different, it would only be because she is my housekeeper for laundry and food. Manja did tell me that if others had not told her about us, she would have let us go our way, as she did not want to put any strain on our happiness. But when others talk about "your husband's girlfriend," she said that she will not stand for it. As much as I blame her, I really can understand how horrible it must be to hear remarks like those.

You could say that my proposal for compromise is the same as it was in Westerbork, but once again Ineke, I don't want that. One thing that you must not forget is that the distress I put you through stemmed from the fact that my relationship with Manja got better, and I became happier while you felt lonely...I would be lonely here even if I saw Manja every day; but maybe I wouldn't feel that way if I knew you trusted me, and I mean one hundred percent!!

I put this compromise before you as an older, and maybe wiser, person, as I feel that it is the most sensible thing for both of us. You know this comes straight from my heart!

It has happened in the last few weeks that both Manja and I feel stronger about an eventual divorce. In these kinds of things, it is so incredibly difficult to decide what would be good and smart. But I do think it would be smart for us to wait a little while.

Even if we don't see each other for the moment, I feel that your presence here, and the possibility of daily contact, is sufficient to get me through this period. Although, maybe even more than you (because you are not working here now), I will miss our getting together.

So my darling, here you have a little idea of the world of my thoughts. Read everything well, think it through well, and then we will talk further.

Kisses from your Jaap

Jaap:

I have to admit that it sounds harsh that I would regard Manja as just my housekeeper for laundry and for food; but the fact is that I was working, and Manja was not. All the married couples in the camp performed whatever tasks were necessary to help each other out.

Ina:

At my first reading of Jaap's letter, I stamped and screamed and swore and cried–all inwardly, of course; for all that it meant was a repeat cycle of the utter exasperation and frustration attached to a relationship that I thought was rapidly becoming too troubling to maintain. After a long while to simmer down, I realized that Jaap was absolutely correct in all his reasonings about taking a definite stand for compromise, even though I hated the thought of unnatural restraints put upon us. I had to reluctantly agree with him about waiting for my parents–after all, life was difficult enough for them without extra aggravation that a scandal would entail. Besides that, I really did want for them to approve of Jaap and understand him to be the fine man that I already knew he was. So I agreed to Jaap's compromise.

Thursday, June 1, 1944

My dearest Sweetheart,

The morning is almost over. I really worked hard and now I am going to chat with you. So we begin our newest period.

Strengthened by everything, I now think that with the start of this period, we should not feel disgruntled. We now know quite well what we have together, and that is a whole lot, though not everything. At least I get to see your pretty face; no one can forbid me that!

Meanwhile it is afternoon, and I was again happy to have seen you for a moment.

It's not so bad that you can't come and visit me now. I'm moving so that the heart patient can get my window bed. I just hope that they don't move me to the top bunk. In any event, I do have a bottom bunk promised to me, and I hope it's not too cramped.

I was so glad to have been able to talk with you in peace for a little while last night, especially because we agreed on everything. I also have real faith in everything, especially in our finding peace together. I have thought that we are not apart here, although it might not appear that way to the outside world.

I am afraid that today's weather isn't too good for you, so I hope that you got some rest. It was real late last night before I got to bed, and this morning I had to get up very early for shaving, so I am extremely tired. Despite the enormous risk, I slept for 15 minutes more, until our Oberscharfuehrer woke me with his hollering screams! Lucky for me it wasn't me he was yelling at. (I had hidden myself rather well), and so I escaped once again. If this had happened yesterday, the results wouldn't have been as good.

So dearest Ineke, that is all the news.

Many, many kisses,

From your Jaap

P.S. 6:00 P.M. and the weather has gotten nasty, and I am getting chills. Hopefully I'm not getting sick. Early to bed tonight with an aspirin.

Bye, my girl,

Jaap

Keep the envelopes in which you receive my letters, and return them to me sometime. I need them.

——— ■　■ ———

Friday, June 2, 1944, 2:15 P.M.

My always dearest Sweetheart,

I just came back from my shower. I'm back here at work, and of course start by not working! You wrote me a great letter yesterday; and I am especially glad that we share the same feelings. I hope you got the message from Josette, and that you understood it. I also told her that Liesje received a package which contained: 1 package of oatmeal, 1 bag of sugar, 3 bars of chocolate, 1 pack of Egyptian cigarettes, 1 piece of soap, 1 tube of toothpaste, and 1 tube of anchovy paste. You can imagine how happy she was, not only with the package, but also with the sign of life, and the fairly recent date (2 weeks ago). It really appears that they know in Amsterdam that we may receive parcels, evidenced in part by the Jewish Council parcels sent by their workers, and we hope that it will be our turn one of these days. I am anxious to know if you are getting any at all.

If you come to work in the *Mutsen Industry*, you will be two rooms away from me; namely, in Room 1, and I am in Room III. In all probability, we then can meet each other once in a while. (Manja works in Room VI). In any event, I think this job would still be the best for your health, compared to the many bad ones. It's not even easy for Manja with all her great contacts!

The IPA's are spreading like wildfire. From now on we will get food every night, and work will stop one hour earlier. We will have to wait and see.

In the meantime, it is pouring outside. I am fortunately sitting where it's warm and dry; but unfortunately, I just heard an announcement that due to the coming visit by the Commission, I *will* have to dig ditches in the camp from 8:00 P.M. until 10:00 P.M. tonight. If you think about me, little one, then at least it might be bearable. I think that I am going to have to move in one or two days. In any event, not tonight, because I must dig!

This afternoon, I went directly from roll call square to the showers, so I assume that you stood there and waited for me in vain.

Meanwhile, an exchange has begun here regarding work; namely, some people have offered to take over tonight's work for a piece of bread. That crazy I am not. Even after such a long day, I can hold out for those two hours. I hope that the weather makes tomorrow night *walkable* so that at least we will be able to say "hello" to each other, and maybe even more. But I am happy enough to see your pretty face from a 50-meter distance, not to mention close up.

See you later then; sleep tight.

Hugs and kisses,

Your Jaap

The Mutsen Industry was a unit where wool-knit caps were torn apart for recycling.

Ina:

In Bergen-Belsen, we could get parcels through the Red Cross from people we knew who were free. My family had friends who had fled to Switzerland. They found out where we were and commissioned the Red Cross to send packages to us.

———■ ■———

Saturday, June 3, 1944

My sweetest darling,

It is now afternoon, and after your visit, I am again in a good mood. Before anything else, I must tell you that everything here is more settled, that we understand each other better, and that we love each other more here than in Westerbork. Your letters testify to this, and as for me, I'm sure you have noticed that it is the same. And so you can well understand how I have longed for you, and how happy I was to have had you with me for a moment, though we really still have to watch out. But we can always find some time, and in that case, we can always say that you need something from my barrack, or that we ran into each other, and then stood talking for a moment. In this way, we can at least have some contact every now and then. Dearest Ineke, I speak here now as an older, wiser, and smarter man, (of course not at heart!), but we must consider the consequences of what we do. You know Manja by now. She is heartless in these matters. She will say that she doesn't want to see me anymore, which on the one hand wouldn't be such a disaster, but on the other hand would create such tremendous difficulties in the practical sense that it could ruin our lives here.

You asked me if I am angry at you for wanting to be so daring, but how can I be mad at such a darling girl who loves me so much! You really are a sweetheart; and if I am mad, it is mostly at myself for having the same desires. But still I want to be, and we must try to be, sensible, because a lovely quarter of an hour between us would be outweighed by all the difficulties it would cause. Hopefully, I will see you for a moment near the entryway tomorrow, (that is, of course, if you just have to visit somebody in the C or D barrack!! - That will be our prearranged excuse in the future.) After that I will take a nap, shave, and then to the usual Sunday concert in Barrack 21. I can think there about the music which we will later enjoy together, and the music will be of much better quality. Then I will eat in the "11," where I will probably stay. In the meantime, it is almost 3:30 P.M., and I have filled up my time with writing to and thinking about you, and in between sleeping and talking have only cut one shoe! Don't be afraid that I am working too hard! So sweetheart, as I was finishing this letter, we just had a whole cabaret with jazz songs at our table. It was great! My afternoon production has risen to cutting four shoes.

Bye, sweet girl of mine. I live on that little kiss we had this afternoon but you may guess what I have in my thoughts. Sleep well tonight.

Kisses,

Your Jaap

Ina:

I was really ready to be *daring* and just flaunt our relationship-and *never mind* Manja, or anyone else. Jaap was obviously more cautious, because it was he who would now suffer the consequences if Manja would ignore him from then on. I could be daring and a winner;he would be a loser in many respects ¡. We had to face the realities of daily life in Bergen-Belsen.

I now felt truly at ease with our decision and my compliance with it. I came to understand my own feelings more clearly; and I dared to express the love

129

that I felt for Jaap. I actually surprised myself with my own honesty, but our surrounding circumstances mocked anything but complete sincerity. How could one mince words or emotions when life was so tenuous and subject to change? I felt calmer and at peace with the situation. Now if we could just live through the agony!

———— ■   ■ ————

Ina:

There was a group of Jews known as the "diamond Jews" in Amsterdam before World War II. Eighty percent of the employers in the diamond trade and 2,100 workers were Jews. The Germans valued their skills, and sought to protect them for their expertise in helping the Germans establish a diamond factory within Bergen-Belsen. To that end, our family and all the other diamond manufacturers and workers were able to avoid deportation to Westerbork for a long period of time, and then eventually transfer to Bergen-Belsen. We were all assigned together to one special barrack in the camp and not allowed to work.

When the factory-planning was initiated, the Germans would convene many meetings often in the middle of the night. I was designated as secretary of the group, since I was the one who could take German shorthand. We would work until deep into the night; and I would take long technical notes on the logistics of the diamond business. The next day, I typed them all out, and much later, donated them to the Dutch Office of War Documentation.

The Germans realized full well that cut stones could bring them much needed foreign currency, thus satisfying their desperate need for industrial diamonds for machine tools. They even transported all needed equipment for operating the factory, although it all remained unused sitting on the train tracks outside the camp.

———— ■   ■ ————

Monday, June 5, 1944

My sweetest darling,

I went to bed pretty early last night (8:30 P.M.), and as I lay there thinking about everything, I felt happy. Which is really crazy because the circumstances at this moment are far from ideal. But yesterday, I was able to speak with you for a moment in peace, after which I saw you a few times; and just the knowledge that there is someone here in this camp whom I love and who loves me, is a peaceful and wonderful feeling. Do you feel it too? I also slept just fine, and had to make do this morning with a handwave from my Ineke in my thoughts! How was it last night? One good thing is that since you have become a secretary, we will have no lack of paper and pencils. As to the latter, I am shortly going to run out, but when that happens, I will give you a signal. In the meantime, see if you can take care of an order for one pencil!

It was really awful in the "21" yesterday afternoon. I left about ten minutes after you did, went with Heinz from Kitchen I, then went to get butter and jam from my barrack, and then to Barrack 21 until 7:00 P.M. Then I went back to my barrack, where fortunately I saw you for a moment, and after that I had a *rich* meal in my barrack. I ate my whole portion of jam, plus the extra food from my Ineke, and then I went to bed satisfied. If you have time tomorrow, maybe you

131

could visit Freddy in his sick bed. He knows everything about us and I think that he would enjoy it–(Barrack 12). In the meantime, I have traded my pajamas for one ration of bread plus six camp-cups full of afternoon meals. The first is for Manja, the last for me. Now I must find out what I can trade next week! Let me know if you know of anyone who wants a white dress shirt, or ties.

I am quite anxious to know how it was last night, of course not so much the internal matters, which are of course a secret, but all the other things, how it went, if it will be something permanent for you. You will be an important person here, won't you?

I am going to keep my bed in the "11C" for sure, and you can understand that I'm glad about that, for more than one reason. The boy in the bunk above me asked me yesterday if I was married to that girl who always comes to visit me. I politely answered that you are a very close friend of mine. But I don't see any harm in remarks like these, because men are so much more cavalier about these things. Don't you think so?

Afternoon, 3:00 P.M.

Now I can continue. I, at least, had a glimpse of my Ineke this afternoon. Tomorrow morning there will be a little hitch in our plans, as after I eat in "11C," I have to go to Barrack 21 and polish off my cup of soup (from the pajamas!). So sweetheart, try to be there when the commando comes on duty, or directly thereafter, but make sure to avoid Manja when she leaves the roll-call square. In any event, we can have ten minutes then. If you can't come because you are eating or something, then let us meet at 6:30 P.M. in my barrack.

The IPA's about the visit of the Commission are spreading like wildfire. Hopefully, at least some of the good things they are saying will be true.

Did you have a concert last night? One of the men at my table was quite enthusiastic about it.

It is now 5:00 P.M., so one and a half hours more, and then we will be one day closer to freedom. I try to reason that way at least once a day.

Maybe I will catch another glimpse of you tonight, otherwise tomorrow afternoon or evening.

Sleep tight, pleasant dreams, many, many kisses,

Your Jaap

Jaap:

Trading for food was common in Bergen-Belsen. Many of the inmates had come to the camp with few or no possessions, so clothes were good trading material. There were occasionally impromptu concerts held in the barracks, and they gave us all a temporary lift.

———■ ■———

Tuesday, June 6, 1944

My dearest Ineke,

I was very happy with our short rendezvous last night. One of these days we will have the opportunity to be together longer. I cannot tell you how glad I am that you have such a great job—first of all, as a diversion, and secondly, that you are rescued from working in the Shoes, Rubber, and other kinds of cleaning.

3:30 P.M.

I was very happy with your visit this afternoon, and even more so with your letter: It fully expresses both our thoughts. It has never been as good between us as it is now; and I also have the true feeling that nothing can change this for the worse, even if the circumstances get nastier.

My sweet darling, for today just this scribble.

Tonight, we will see each other again.
Lots of love and kisses,
Your Jaap

———■ ■———

June 7, 1944, 8:30 P.M.

My dearest Ineke,

Just a few words from my bed. Remember darling, be smart and don't get sick; we just can't have that here. If it happened, I would have to violate all strict rules and set foot in Barrack 17!! Everybody is all excited about the invasion, and of course I am too, mostly because at moments such as these our future becomes tangible. I, of course, had my dreams before, but everything seemed so far away. Now it is as if our chances are closer at hand, and along with that, come all the optimistic thoughts that I had for a happy future for both of us. Do you feel that too, darling? Maybe it is extra good that we feel this way, because it will get harder for us here by the day, with each success of the English. I had a small example here today at the shoe factory where you could feel the Germans' lousy moods; but it is especially then that my ties with you make it so much easier to carry on. I am dead tired; so only these few thoughts for you. Sleep sweetly, be all healthy tomorrow, much, much love and kisses,

Your Jaap

———■ ■———

Thursday, June 8, 1944

My sweetest darling,

Hopefully, you are feeling somewhat better. I was really worried about you. This morning I was very unlucky, in that I had to haul shoes outside of the tent, of course resulting in my getting drenched. Hopefully, I can get out of it this afternoon. What do you say about the fact that *the Palestinians have to start working? It doesn't look good for them. There was no further invasion news this morning, so sweet darling, until tonight. I'm writing this little epistle in the outhouse, not the most suitable place for concentrating. All the best, sweetheart.

Many, many kisses and love,

Your Jaap

*Inmates promised passage to Palestine were awaiting their trip as exchange prisoners.

———■　■———

Friday, June 9, 1944

My dearest Ineke,

I think that we both look forward so much to our short rendezvous; and you cannot imagine how great it is for me after such a long day to have the knowledge that you are here, that you think of me, that you love me; and that at the end of the day I can see you even if only for a short time. It gives me the courage I need to carry on. When I had to work here in those first few months, everything was much more arduous, because I only hoped that I would see you again. And now that everything has become a reality, we both should find the courage from each other to get through the difficult times which are undoubtedly ahead of us, and which we will hopefully survive together.

And now I am going to sleep darling. In my thoughts I kiss and hug you.

Your Jaap

———■   ■———

Sunday, June 11, 1944

My sweetest Darling,

I am already in bed, but am using a large book as a writing pad. I said to you a mere fifteen minutes ago that you would get something from me in writing, and so I keep my promise, (didn't I do that quickly?) I was a bit frustrated that my intended visit today fell through, although we really shouldn't complain about a day such as today. I am glad that you got rid of your fever so quickly, but take care that it stays that way. Watch your intestines, you understand? Do you know that in my mind I was already afraid that you'd have to go into the hospital where I could only visit you once a week on Wednesday evenings? Freddy, my brother-in-law, has jaundice, and was taken to the hospital today. It will take him at least four weeks to get better. I really don't think that Manja has any idea about our regular contact, but the strange thing is, I'm not afraid of an eventual discovery, because I really believe that Our Good Lord is with us. On the other hand, we should not think that nothing could happen to us, with regard to what we are doing, so we should not overdo it. So, as soon as you are better, (let us assume Tuesday!), let us limit ourselves to our daily visits in our *cozy corner*.

In the meantime, they got me out of bed twice. The first time it was Ernst, who brought me a small cup of lunch food from Liesje. Don't I have a nice sister who remembers her brother in this way? Then they got me out of bed for two extra spoonsful of rhubarb, which was also worth it. Now it is almost 9:00 P.M., and I'm beginning to get tired.

Till tomorrow night: (a long time away).

Many, many kisses and love,

Your Jaap

———■ ■———

Saturday, June 17, 1944

My dearest Ineke,

I can't tell you how bad I feel for you about yesterday.... It won't happen very often, but that it happened this time is too much. What others say about me doesn't interest me at all, because I just know that in the worst case they will later say that my role was not so bad after all. Additionally, these gossiping people do not interest me because most of them are not blameless themselves, and deep in their hearts are only sorry that they cannot be blamed for something. Do you understand me? In any event, there's only one important thing for us both, and that is that we love each other, and that we can trust each other. I am satisfied with our afternoon meetings. You too? We at least feel some peace in this unpeaceful camp; and these meetings also give me hope for a good future for us together, even if we don't say much. What do you think about our being together in a quiet little house in the winter time by a hearth after a delicious meal? I really almost can't imagine that there will ever be such happiness in store for us! So sweet child, I'm going back to my barbed wire; but whether it be ballplaying, tearing up shoes, or barbed wire, my thoughts still stay with you. I am anxious to see if it will be the same later when I am working, but of course then I will have a picture of Ineke on my desk! - As you see, these are only dreams of the future!

Till tonight, many, many kisses,

Your Jaap

———■　■———

Tuesday, June 20, 1944, 4:45 P.M.

My dear darling,

Just a few words in compensation for missing our quarter of an hour. I indeed missed it very much, but since you are such an important woman, I must put up with it. Although on the one hand I feel sorry for you that you have to work so hard; on the other hand, I am very happy for you that you have this distraction, that you are busy, and also, that it is interesting. And thus, we must miss our quiet rendezvous every once in awhile. I am also very anxious to know what will become of all this. I count on the fact that you and your parents will at least have a Palestine Certificate as a back-up, just in case bad things (which we don't count on) might happen. As to that, I think that they are just trying to frighten us.

I am now lying on my bed feeling wonderful, with my face in the sun, and I feel satisfied about this day. Think of when we will be able to go out at night together. When will that happen for the first time, darling? Everybody is crazy here because the Inspection Committee is coming back. I can't wait to see what will happen.

Darling, try to steal a pencil for me somewhere! You, with your great contacts, may be able to obtain such a thing. Did you know that I'm really proud of you, that you do everything so well? So my girl, after this short talk, I must start working again. I have to study the Dutch language which I have to teach to the boys tomorrow. In any case, it is very nice that all the boys in my shoe group want this.

Darling, I hope till tonight, otherwise definitely till tomorrow. Many, many kisses and love,

Jaap

P.S. 6:30 P.M.–I'm beginning to get very pessimistic about seeing you today. I'm going to look at your picture tonight. Until tomorrow, darling.

> *Jaap*:
> My friends and I set up a very informal school in the shoe factory to distract ourselves from the mind-numbing work we had to do. Whenever we could work it in, during breaks and meals, we would take the risk of holding classes.

——— ■ ■ ———

Wednesday, June 21, 1944

My dearest Ineke,

I am sitting here so close to you; but as it should be, I will not bother you while you are working. Besides, the stern look your uncle gave me is enough to keep me away. I really hope that you can take a few days off soon, as you will need it badly. I was so glad to have spoken to you last night; I really had the feeling that you would come out, and just when I had given up hope, you promptly did come out! I slept well (which I really shouldn't mention to you), and made use of the air raid to make up my report for Albala, and to learn the language problems that I have to teach this afternoon. I am getting a group of 20 boys, 11 years old, and will teach them arithmetic, languages, history, and a general view on business, art, and science, for 1½ hours, and then another half-hour of talk about various subjects. There is such an annoying lack of books here, but I think I might have enough material. I just hope that you have five minutes for me later in our quiet corner. The tables have really turned now: In Westerbork I was so busy, and you had so much time; and here I must wait quietly until my Ineke has a few minutes for me. It's not so bad, you understand. I'm just glad that you have something to do, even if you have to work so hard, because it is at least a completely different type of hard work than any other commando here in Celle.

Love from your Jaap

Ina:

We had air raid alarms regularly. When the Germans were alerted that planes were coming, the sirens sounded, and all the laundry lines outside had to be cleared right away. We washed our one change of clothing ever so often in the available cold water, but there was nowhere to let them dry inside. After the all-clear, there was always a mad scramble to get back to the lines to re-hang the wet things. If you were too late to find space there, then you were forced to spread them wet under your mattress.

Jaap:

Albala was known as the "camp elder," a Greek Jew who was in charge of our section of the camp, the Sternlager, which was sometimes even called *Albalalager*. Albala was not liked by us at all. He was very chummy with the Germans, and would always walk alongside the SS during roll-call. He was always beautifully dressed in a sport coat and a shirt, and his wife dressed well too. They had a young son who was also beautifully garbed, and looked like a little prince.

In the end, his little boy died on the train to Troebitz, and I buried him. I think Albala was prosecuted after the war, but they weren't too hard on him because of his great loss.

The Jewish camp leaders could switch people's work around if they wished. They knew that I had been principal of the school in Westerbork, and there was no school in Bergen-Belsen. Most of the children had been deported to death camps, so their numbers here were limited to those children of people who held papers of privilege.

Ina:

I remember that experience with my uncle. One time, we were eating our lunch soup from our bowls outside because the weather was lovely. Uncle Hans and my sister were there, and Jaap passed by; and I either waved at him or looked at him in a certain way, because my uncle looked at me and asked a kind of suspicious question which implied, "Is something going on between you two?" It must have suddenly dawned on him. I thought, "Now he knows."

———■ ■———

Wednesday, June 21, 1944, 10:00 P.M.

My dearest Ineke,

I made use of the fact that I still have Manja's fountain pen in my possession to write another letter to you, so that in this way maybe, our respective descendants can preserve them. As it is already late, I won't write much. First of all, you are my sweet darling. This you already are, but after I get a little note from you like I did today, that proves it to me again. This letter shows your exact inner feelings, and that is just great. That there is a difference between my letters in Westerbork and here also makes sense, because fortunately, my feelings here are more positive, and I know what I want. I had another long talk with Manja tonight, in a truly friendly tone, and the only really bad part was that I had to walk with my arm around her. But first of all, Manja would walk that way with almost anyone, so most certainly with me; and secondly, it is difficult for me to refuse her arm! What we discussed, later. In the meantime, it is getting quite late. I played chess in one competition for the championship of the barrack. I won one and lost one. Sweet lady of mine, it is getting dark.

Till tomorrow,

Many, many kisses,

your Jaap

Ina:

That Manja insisted on walking with arms entwined, meant nothing special to me. That was very much a part of her normal behavior. As nasty as she could be, she always acted in a very affectionate way as part of her normal approach to people. She was, what would be called today, a *touchy-feely* person, literally, and, at moments of benign feelings, always expressed herself with many endearing words:

142

darling, sweetheart, etc., in a kind of admiring and loving way–even towards me in the "good" times.

———■　■———

Friday, June 23, 1944

My dearest lady,

Just a little talk with you from my new living quarters. It is now 8:30 P.M., which is quite early for me, and I am settled here, in any event decently enough for me to have female visitors. And although we will be somewhat less free than in that quiet corner, it may also be possible for us to be able to speak to one another here in peace. I often think about how what we are doing is so directly out of line with the sensible words I wrote to you after my argument with Manja. You do understand why I go on seeing you, and both you and I know that it makes us happy, and because of this, life here is so much more bearable for us than for so many others. I tell you quite honestly that I am not at all afraid of being discovered. We will get out of it at that time, and I am not going to have something taken away that is building up so nicely, and that has so much promise. So if we are found out, we must then act as understanding people who don't want bad feelings to prevail. I can already see that this will not be easy, because I see that as our ties become closer here, it will be more and more difficult for us to wait until after the war. But still I believe that this is of mutual interest. Now, sweet Ineke, I hope that as you finish reading these few words, you are lying in the arms of Morpheus. I must approve of this, even though I would much prefer to have my arms in his place. Sleep well and long, and I plan to do the same.

Till tomorrow, darling,

Your Jaap

———■　■———

Thursday, June 29, 1944

My dearest love,

Of course from my new, although actually old job, a letter. I don't feel very well, but hope to feel better soon enough. I'm at a nice table with people I know, which helps a lot. With all our talking, the afternoon goes fairly quickly (it is already 5:30 P.M.). Not that we work too hard, because all I cut is one shoe all afternoon. A record!! What do you say to the fact that all the Palestine Certificate holders got to take off their Jewish stars? It can only mean something good, and I really hope that, in spite of everything, it will be our turn soon too.....I think that for you, the removal of the Jewish star should convince you that a transport such as this is a far better choice than a "diamond town," which at this point is merely fiction! One thing that is difficult about being surrounded by so many people, is that they all ask me what I'm doing sitting here and writing. Just now, a new IPA about our Palestine Papers. I am very curious, and hope to hear the truth very soon from you about your papers. Yes, darling! I am beginning to believe in the forward motion of this whole business. It is just too bad that our quiet afternoon hours have again been denied us. We will still make something good out of it, of that I am sure. I just now got a permit for the barber's, so darling, tomorrow you will find your man who is 31, looking much older than that, with a clean shaven head. I'll look at least 41! Will you still look at me then? I spoke to Liesje again, and as a departing gesture, she gave me two cigarettes and a bread knife. She really is a darling sister, and I am incredibly glad that she is the first of all of us to go. She really deserves it with her love for Israel. I want to go to bed early tonight, notwithstanding my haircut and eventual Palestine registration. I'm dead tired, which is probably because of the heat, as it is very muggy here.

See you later.

Many, many kisses, Jaap

144

Jaap:

The Germans agreed to send 222 Zionists to Palestine in exchange for a group of German citizens interned there. Most of those in the exchange were elderly, but my sister Liesje was lucky enough to be included as a nurse. All other Palestine Certificate holders thought their turns would be next, but there were no other transfers or transports to Palestine for the remainder of the war.

———■ ■———

Friday, June 30, 1944

My dearest darling,

Even if it is terribly noisy in the afternoon, and even if there are too many gaps in our seeing each other, such as happened this afternoon, I still think it is wonderful to know that you are near me. I have hardly done anything this afternoon, and I feel quite good, much less tired than yesterday, also probably because the weather is less warm; and so I am completely satisfied in my new hovel! But I heard this afternoon that we will have to stay here for the moment, as we cannot leave until the Albanians who are in Number 10 go to work. All I can do is keep cutting shoes. I started to learn Spanish this afternoon. In fact, I want to spend some time every day on language studies, which is quite possible at this table with so many knowledgeable people. A great improvement over my last table. If I should forget to ask you later, are you still thinking about my "necktie business?" Whatever I get for them is that little bit extra, since I won't wear them here. Eventually, we will go together and buy a new collection of your choice in Amsterdam or Tel Aviv! Bye darling, till later,

Many, many kisses
your Jaap

Saturday, July 1, 1944, 5:30 P.M.

My dear girl,

For today only a small Shabbat note. It was nice and quiet here today, and we had long discussions about returning home after the war, reparations for our losses, etc. In your last letter you touched upon the important matter of what our situation will be after the war. There are so many problems here that it is almost impossible to point at a good solution for us together. Just think about it. Problem 1:–Will we end up in the same place, let us assume Amsterdam; and if not, how long will it take for us to come together there or elsewhere? 2:–How long will it take for me to get a divorce, and what will Manja think of our relationship after the war? 3:–Financial position; which will force me to start working hard immediately, which I will do with pleasure. But will we, and this is the 4th, and the most important thing: in this new and I hope everlasting period, not let anything stand in our way? For that, we will really have to get to know one another, although that may sound crazy, but you understand what I mean. Sweet darling, this subject isn't meant to be discussed in this way on this little piece of paper. So we will talk quietly about all of these problems one of these days, either privately, or in a long "shoe-letter." Bye darling; do you still think a little bit about me on such a long day?

Many, many kisses and love,
your Jaap

P.S.   I forgot to put down problem No. 5-Rudi. I believe there are more problems, but I still am convinced that everything will turn out fine!

Ina:

This was the first time that Jaap alluded to Rudi Acohen as a "problem" for us. Heretofore, I had always been the one to bring him up short on this whenever he seemed to become too enthusiastic about our future together, ignoring, (or conveniently forgetting), that Rudi and I were unofficially engaged before the war. Rudi and I were childhood friends from the time we met when our families were vacationing at a summer resort. I was twelve and he was thirteen. That friendship eventually turned into a romance.

Rudi and his family were arrested by the Germans in a raid in June 1942, when he was 20 years old. At that time, I was totally ignorant of what really happened after he was sent to "the East". In fact, I even sent a registered letter to him in Auschwitz for which I received a receipt signed by a German official; but I never heard any more after that. According to records, he and his family died three months after their arrest.

———■ ■———

Monday, July 3, 1944, 8:00 A.M.

My dearest Ineke,

As I half expected, our walk didn't work out last night because just when I was going to see you, as you were going to the wash room, Manja came back. I hope you slept well, since you looked dead tired. I slept well on my lower bunkbed next to the window: that is the best place, but the other circumstances have not improved. There are now 220 people in our Barrack, so there's an awful lot of traffic; and, for us, I believe it means being more careful. Honestly, I think it would be better if we meet and sit outside, at least when the weather is good, rather than inside on my bed, which always gives more of an impression of intimacy. Maybe it is an even better idea for us only to meet once a day either in the afternoon or in the evening. Yes, my dear, here we are again in another new situation, as Belsen always presents new aspects. Truthfully, as unpleasant as this is for us now, just the fact that there are changes makes life more bearable, as it breaks the monotony. If I write to you now that we must be more careful and sensible, I think you know why. For a few weeks now, things have gone quite well, and we have to be thankful for that; but you know, that despite all the happy meetings, many negative things could have come out of it. We must see to it that we avoid this, and though we don't want to, we will have to give up some of those already too short half-hours together. Do you feel the same about all this, sweetheart? In the meantime, there are more than enough IPA's. Last evening, I had a nice meal with Liesje from her Red Cross parcel sent to those leaving for Palestine: eight thin slices of bread with respectively, cocoa, sugar, *curbis*, with thick butter and canned salmon. What do you say to that? This piece of paper is now almost full. Maybe this afternoon more, with better contents.

Much, much love
your Jaap

———■　■———

Tuesday, July 4, 1944, 5:00 P.M.

My dearest girl,

I am writing you a letter this afternoon, because I succeeded at getting work in the shoe factory again. Of course I am very happy about it, because at least it gives me some quiet time to talk with you in my thoughts and in writing. Beppo, our leader, took care of it for me, and his birthday is tomorrow; so since he has been really nice to us all, we will present him with a tie.

I hope that you had a chance to sleep this afternoon. I saw how tired you were, - no wonder with this warm weather which I hope is over now. Last night I slept very badly because of the heat and the lice; and I really hope that doesn't happen again as I am dead tired after the last two nervewracking days.

So darling, see you soon.

Many, many kisses,
Jaap

———■　■———

Curbis: a gourd, used as a decorative fruit; belongs to the pumpkin family. Almost inedible.

Wednesday, July 5, 1944, 5:00 P.M.

My dearest Ineke,

For today a little bit more than usual, only due to the fact that our meeting today was so short. Sweet darling, I agree with you that the situation has become better for us, because first of all, we have grown closer together, but furthermore, that those little visits on the top bunk, sometimes with the pleasure of a special gourmet treat (meaning the two full portions of camp food which you laid out for us, and only special because you arranged it!!), were really nice. The afternoon here has passed quietly; I even got some work done, but finally I am now doing the most important work! One of these days, it will be time to sort your letters again, as they have slowly become a respectable package. I am very anxious to know about the 108 Jewish Council packages which arrived, and I only hope that I have a chance to get one. After all this ordinary talk, again some of my thoughts about you, me, us. I think you are such a darling girl. That you know of course; but every once in a while, I want to tell you again, otherwise you might think that I'm taking you for granted. Then, that I like to go to bed nice and early like you do, and so that can be added to the many points that our characters have in common. Do you still remember how, in our long talks in Westerbork, this similarity became the basis for a possible future life together? It is very important to note that we have almost never had an argument, which is mostly because of our similarities; and maybe also because I am older than you. That's perhaps why you adapt yourself more easily to my thinking, but I really don't think this last thing to be true, so it must be the former and not the latter! You still have to tell me how things were with your former *lovers*, in terms of character similarities. Of course you cannot really compare, because the life in which we find ourselves is not a normal one. In the meantime, it is almost 6:00 P.M., and I had to participate in a debate about Orthodoxy. You know my feelings about this, and here we also agree! Go to bed early tonight, as you looked tired this afternoon. I'm going to shave, and hope to be in bed by 9:00 P.M.

Much, much love,

your Jaap

Jaap:

Although Ina and I were both raised as Orthodox Jews, we were both quite cynical about the pious Jews who continued to practice under the most abhorrent conditions. What good would it do to be Kosher–and dead!

———■ ■———

Ina:

Jaap had fallen ill with one of his many bouts of *Kampziekte–camp sickness*, a form of typhoid that plagued most everyone in Bergen-Belsen one time or another. Three days of a very high fever, terrible diarrhea, throwing up, not being able to eat–and all of a sudden, you would feel better. The big problem was to get your strength back, because it was so debilitating. But on what? When I had it, my sister saved up my rations of bread and margarine, and she would have it for me when I would wake up ravenous one morning and say, "Oh my God, I'm so hungry." When you're that ill, you don't get your strength back from so little food, and that's what happened to so many people. They contracted typhoid fever over and over, and just wasted away.

———■ ■———

Saturday, July 8, 1944

My dearest darling,

It is now 10:00 A.M., I have just slept for an hour, and now I am going to chat with you. I feel fine, but must of course give the right impression, so I am boiling hot with a red scarf around my neck. Last night 100.9°, this morning 99.5°, so a downward trend. But they'll give me a few more days at least, and I am very comfortable here. I see now how different life here really is when you're not working hard; and when you get some rest, you find out how exhausted you really are. I divide my day between eating, sleeping, and reading. As to the latter, I have already read three books, of which yours was the best: "The Man Without a Soul", and "Life Goes On"–the titles tell you everything. But good enough for in bed. As for "Clementine" and "The Man Without a Soul", Manja bartered them for me in the "21" barrack. I have very nice exchange material, and you only get books if you also have books to give out. In addition, tonight at 8:00 P.M., we're getting a "radio announcement" from Dr. Elias, who will then inform us of all the official and unofficial news: first political, the Camp news, then the food situation, very cleverly done, with his own commentary on the IPA's. The fall of Vilna was reported to us by IPA. In the meantime, consider this as a first letter from someone who has been very ill and is writing some ordinary news from his sickbed. I will forgive you your short hairdo, first of all, because the weather is warm; secondly, I can't be mad at you anyway; and third, and most important, I have to see the results first. But I'll say again that a pretty face stays a pretty face!

Many, many kisses and love,
your Jaap

Jaap:

Vilna in Lithuania had an active Jewish community before the war. In the summer of 1941, 35,000 out of nearly 100,000 Jews were murdered there by the Germans, and a ghetto was set up there for the remaining Jews. There was a dramatic resistance effort in the ghetto, but the area was liquidated anyway in September 1943.

Dr. Elias used to pretend he was a radio announcer, and would entertain us by telling us all the IPA's floating around the camp.

———■　■———

Sunday, July 9, 1944

My dear girl,

What time are you going to the dentist tomorrow? If I am sleeping, make sure you wake me up right away. This morning 96.4° so .... The doctor was just here; my throat is 100%! No fever, so, normally, I would have been released immediately, if it weren't for the fact that at the moment there are no releases because there is no room in the barracks. So I am going to stay here a little longer. It is 1:00 P.M., and we are all eagerly awaiting the food about which there has been a big rumor. It is supposed to be terrible. But I am so hungry that I'm sure I'll eat it. I just got up and will go and eat sitting at the table. I am writing in several parts. It is now 1:30 P.M., I just shoved down the food–there are no other words I can find to describe it; but for heaven's sake, there is nothing we can do about it! I also just received your letter and food: I will do my best to keep it till tonight, and am in complete agreement with the way in which you bargain! But for 2 cigarettes, it really wasn't worth it. They are throwing away the food here! I've never had any as bad as

153

it was today, but you are right that we shouldn't complain when you hear the stories about the Albanians, who have it much worse. Luckily, I will be able to complete my afternoon meal with 2 slices of Dutch bread and biscuits due to the arrival of the long awaited Jewish Council parcel. Although receiving bread, biscuits, oatmeal, grease drippings, and sugar cubes, it is not a large supply, as we have to divide everything with Liesje and her children; but we are very happy as this shows that we have not been forgotten. Enclosed is a "taste" from the package. Eat it to the health of both of us. Now the following: I hope to be free at 7:00 P.M., to be at the window on the side of Barrack 18, (pretty close to the end). If you can be there then, maybe we will be able to talk to each other, if it is possible to open the window; otherwise, in any case, tomorrow as I hope to be getting up. I've had things I wanted to write for two days now; but as crazy as it sounds, I never get to it. Maybe this afternoon. Bye sweetheart. Many, many kisses and love,

    your Jaap

Jaap:

The food situation was really deteriorating badly now. The German Kitchen, Kitchen No. 1, where I worked for the last nine months in the camp, cooked for the SS and the privileged inmates in the beginning. But after three or four months there, they also got the same dreadful food. Almost all the Albanians, who also lived in the Sternlager, died. They kept the Jewish dietary laws; and because there was sometimes a little horsemeat in the soup, they wouldn't eat it. Some of them were shipped to Auschwitz later on; they were all in very bad shape by then.

———■ ■———

Sunday, July 9, 1944

My dearest Ineke,

You are probably wondering where my letter is, but I gave it to Freddy at 12:00 P.M., who didn't really have any time till this afternoon to get away, and hopefully, by now you have received it. I feel good. My evening temperature was 99.6°, so not too high. In short, I consider each day here a real treat. It's just fantastic that you received parcels from Tel Aviv, and there is an actual real chance that there might be an exchange due to the letters from Vienna. I believe that means that we are sitting here with the best possible papers. Here they are talking about the delay in this evening's soup, and that instead we are going to get tins of beets, one for each of 3 people. I don't find that a very profitable trade off, but we will have to wait and see. I wrote a letter asking to get out of my outside commando job when I'm released from the hospital, and am now waiting to hear. Don't pay attention to your English *teacher* when he wants to correct your pronunciation. If you yourself know what's right, and also know that he doesn't know, then just let it give you some good satisfaction. I have to stop because Freddy has to take this. Have a restful night, sleep well.

Many, many goodnight kisses,
your Jaap

———■   ■———

Tuesday, July 11, 1944, 10:30 A.M.

My dearest Sweetheart,

For today, just a short letter about *our* problems. You asked me a few days ago how I would take it if your love for someone else turned out to be stronger than it is for me. Yes darling, that is indeed a difficult point that we can and must talk about because as we get to know each other, we have to know that these risks do exist, with you maybe even more than me because of Rudi. There is a chance here of a great disappointment, I hope you understand, on either side. I would take it......as a man (that sounds funny), and you should never make an eventual decision just to avoid bringing me pain. Of course, the situation could be reversed; but I know that the disappointment I would cause would be very miserable for you. I am not saying that it wouldn't be the same for me, to the contrary; but a man can always counteract his feelings with his work, (also with other women, but that is not for me). For a woman, it is much more difficult. The worst would be, if after, let us say, six months, when we know each other well, and know what we want, Rudi, who still has a part of your heart, (and I must say that I can't blame you for this), returns home. Then you will have to see how you adjust to him, with the added factor of you not wanting to hurt somebody who has already gone through so much sorrow. In the meantime, this old man of yours is getting older. I am now seeing everything pessimistically, which we have to every once in awhile; but dear Ineke, I am an optimist about our relationship, and believe that a great deal can come out of it. Let us hope that all the difficulties, which we will no doubt have to face in many forms, will be overcome by our love, which will then be the basis for the start of a very strong marriage.

Bye, sweetheart.

Kisses, your Jaap

Ina:

Every now and then, emotions about Rudi, though usually sublimated, would well up and overtake all other feelings. The truth was that I missed him. I remembered all the youthful banter and fun we would have that seemed to have happened in another lifetime; and I regretted that those times would never return again. I felt sorry for our unfulfilled love, and I truly felt conflicted about the new feelings I had for Jaap. They were so different from anything that Rudi and I ever shared. I thought it would be unfair for me not to air these doubts with Jaap. I did; and he could not be more understanding. His attitude always reinforced my admiration for him. Therefore I made as much of a commitment to Jaap as my heart would allow me to, without making myself feel guilty and unfair to Rudi. It was a matter of compassion and loyalty as well as sheer decency to be considering the consequences of Rudi's possible return. After all, it was taken for granted before the war that we would be together as a couple; but as the upheavals occurred all around us, I had a pervasive, deep down feeling of doom. It clouded my resolve to think only one way, and I persuaded myself to allow the possibility of a decision later on as events unfolded. I felt very strongly attached to Jaap, and I did not want to lose him either.

———■　■———

Wednesday, July 12, 1944

My dearest Ineke,

Do you know what I wanted to do this afternoon–to crawl into bed with you and take a nap together. But for the moment, these are only wishes and dreams. You really looked very tired, and I hope that in the meantime you had a good sleep. I also took it easy. It is now 3:15 P.M., and I am writing this little epistle at the dentist. At 4:00 P.M., roll call, and then the afternoon is over, thus putting us one day closer to the freedom in our future. The crazy thing is, that despite all optimistic reports and outlooks, when I hear about this future, which seems to be really close at hand, I don't feel that it's really true. Not that I have given up hope that we will get out of it, but the way I feel is that we are not there by a long shot. Let us hope that my feelings are wrong. But just because I feel this way, it doesn't mean I can't work out the problems of the future. The most important thing is, in the first place, the basis on which Manja and I will stay together in the beginning; and respectively, how we will then separate. I will first discuss this with her. How do I think it should be? Both of us living like friends, with regular contact. Then there are the problems with the families, who we hope will come back; for instance the furniture that we have to gather together and divide. And last, but not least, the abandoning of our marriage vows, even though we are still married, and the granting each other full personal freedom. Don't you too think that this is the best way to clearly define everything?

See you later: (I still love you, you know!)
Many, many kisses,
your Jaap

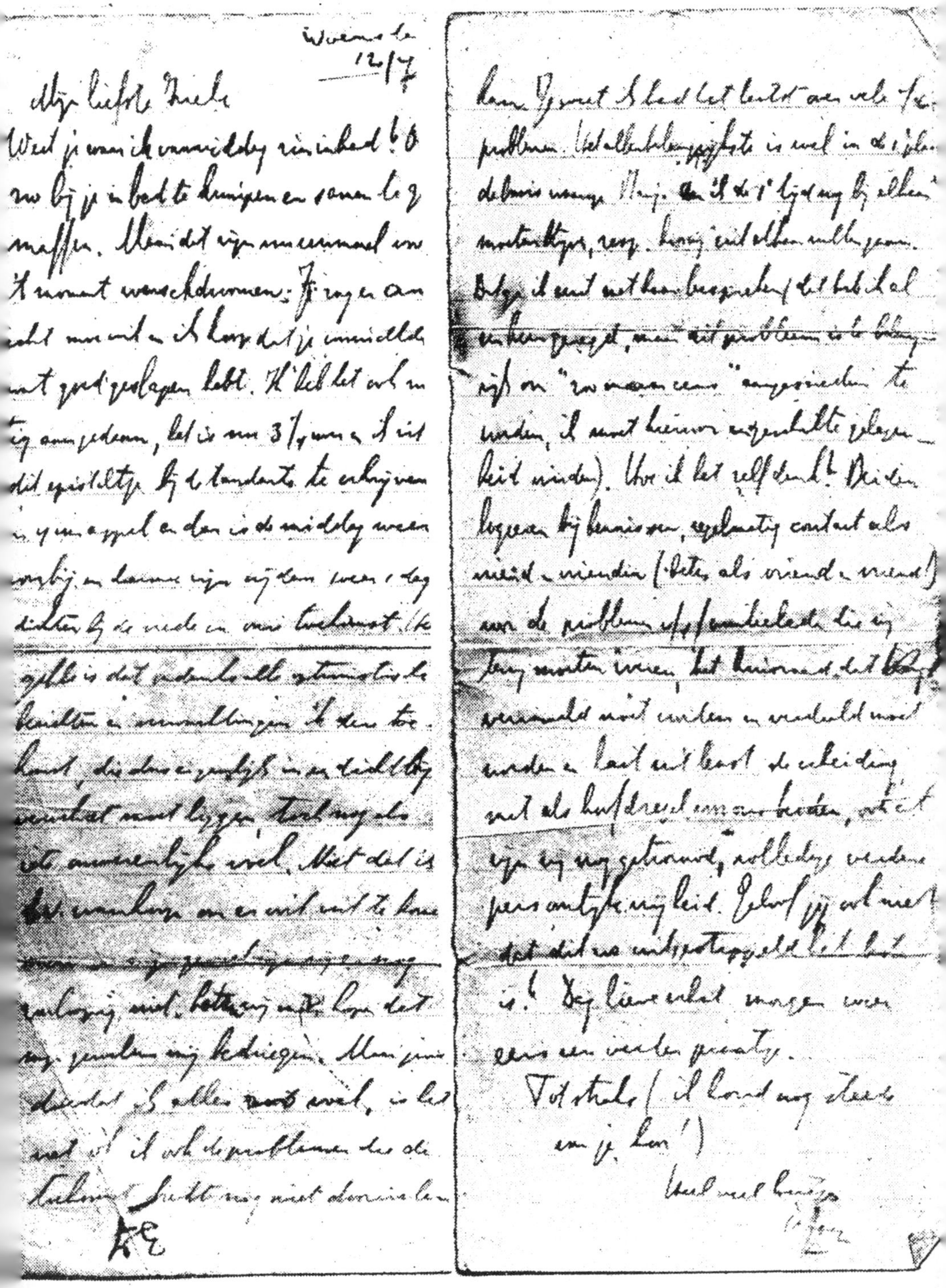

*Monday, July 17, 1944 (I happen to remember this date quite well!)

Jaap:
I will never forget this date: the day I was released in Amsterdam, (July 17, 1942), after being arrested in a raid and almost shot.

My dear Ineke,

I am using this roll call as an opportunity to write to you while standing in one of the last rows under a few lights. Not that I have that much to write. As bad as our contact is, it becomes satisfactory for us just to keep busy with the little daily annoyances we have here. The crazy thing is that the big problems that keep us busy are all so vague because we don't know yet what will happen with this world that is giving us these problems. I often have the feeling that any conversation about all of this is only theoretical. So for the moment, we must be satisfied with this stupid life of eating, sleeping, and talking about things which in our normal lives wouldn't even be worth discussing; and also face the fact that contact such as we had in Westerbork in those first months is impossible here. Sweetheart, this is only a little roll call contemplation, nothing special, but every so often I really enjoy writing to you, even if only for the pleasure I know it gives you. Bye, darling of mine, see you later.

Many, many kisses and love,
your Jaap

*_A full account of this day is included in The Early Years._

Ina:

The roll call ritual was one of the most cruel and miserable experiences we had to endure in the camps. The people who went to work in the morning assembled in a central field and were first to be counted in rows of five deep, ten wide—just squares of humanity. When the same people returned from work, they had to go on roll call again. We, from the diamond group did it only once a day, but it very often lasted several hours in all kinds of weather. The Germans counted us, then went into the barracks and counted the mothers with small children who stood by their beds, as well as the sick ones in bed. The total number of people outside and inside had to tally for each barrack. Sometimes, we felt that they just said the numbers were not correct while we stood there, hour after hour, in the rain, in the icy cold, the snow, or the blistering heat. At the same time, they would inspect the beds to see that they were militarily perfect. If not, they would pull the bedding apart, order the luckless one to do it over, and deprive that person of bread rations. They did not check for cleanliness, only to be sure that the beds were made up properly. I had a bed next to a woman who had a little blond baby boy, and the woman who checked our beds had her own little boy at home. She was so touched when she saw this baby, that she would play with him and forget to look at the beds most of the time. We were lucky.

Jaap:

We were standing endlessly in the worst weather, (those of us who could stand), never at ease, for 2 or 3 hours; and you would have to be very careful how you looked, where you looked. You could not look the SS guards in the eye, because you might be hit at any moment by the butt of a rifle.

———■　■———

Jaap:

There was a long period of approximately six weeks during which I was unable to write to Ina because I had another job working in the better of the two kitchens. When there was an announcement that they needed workers again, I reported for duty, and the Oberscharfuehrer said to me: "Didn't I see you before?" And I said, "Yes, but this time I will do better. I will make sure that nothing will happen this time." Kitchen No. 1 was the best food-work to be had. Out of Kitchen No. 2 came the dreadful soup and imitation coffee that the rest of the camp got. I worked for almost 9 months in the kitchen. I had to leave my barrack at 3:00 a.m. and didn't return until 8:00 P.M.; and although it was terribly exhausting work, at least I had the benefit of eating better than others, and being able to steal bits of food also. I used to steal sugar in an old sock, which I would conceal inside my underwear.

The Oberscharfuehrer's name was Heinz, and he was a real son-of-a-bitch. I remember I was once finished with work and ready to go back to my barrack and had just stolen a slab of butter. Right

162

then, Heinz came in and said, "Hey you, stir that vat," at which point I quickly hid the butter inside my workpants. Rapidly, the butter began to melt from the intense heat. Fortunately, he left, but I'll never forget the feeling of the butter running down my leg, and how afraid I was that I'd be caught.

Ina:

When Manja was ill with *kampziekte*, I would go out and make Jaap's bed for him. I would always find an onion, some sugar, or some salt hidden inside the sheet. Usually, I would find a note and leave a note. I remember that when Jaap came back late at night, and the lights were already out in my barrack, he would somehow find me in my bed and give me a quick goodnight kiss.

———■　■———

Friday, September 1, 1944

My dear, dear lady,

Just a few little words to which you really have a right after so many months of silence. I make use of the opportunity of having to wait in the hospital to write to you for a moment, only to tell you that I believe I love you as much as you love me, and that we have the same desire for each other. And these are the things, which in these last months to come, (I hope I'm not being too pessimistic), will keep us on our feet. We will come through this, dearest Ineke, and then you will see that we will have a lovely time together. Then we can say that our will to survive was not in vain. My coming to see you depends on the work I have. If I can, I will go straight to bed and speak with you tomorrow, I hope long enough; but at least you can see me for a minute, but I really don't want another........

(this letter is unfinished)

———■ ■———

Sunday, September 3, 1944, 5:30 P.M.

My Ineke,

I am not at all satisfied with our mail service, as I've had a letter waiting for you already since 2:00 P.M., but Freddy was only here for a short while, and with Manja, so I couldn't give it to him. Later, I will give him both letters. In the meantime, they have brought in the first patient from the new transport. I hope that doesn't continue, or I will be out of here fast. I will tell Josette what time I will be at the fence tomorrow, and then we will at least talk to each other again. They just took away the new patient that they had brought in. They're not taking anyone from the new transport. Someone said that they are all from Budapest, or with Palestine papers, or of double nationalities. I am anxious to know what the truth is. I just tried to eat something, but after two bites I was so sick that I, along with many others here, had to throw away a whole campbowl full of food. Absolute pig food! How, my Ineke, I myself could swallow almost one portion, *almost one whole portion*, is a complete mystery to me.

I just asked for Josette, because I found out that Freddy is sick and can't come. Josette however, has not shown up yet, and thus it looks as if there is no possibility of contact today. Tomorrow, in any case, will be better.

Goodnight, sweetheart. Tell me again how you feel, as you did not write that.

Many, many goodnight kisses,

your Jaap

———■　■———

Thursday, September 28, 1944

My dearest sweetheart,

Still sick: I had a terrible night's sleep. This morning 100°, this afternoon 100.9°, and I am afraid that it's going up. Furthermore, Manja visited me, and I bluntly told her the truth; and that, in combination with my illness, in all probability, brought peace again. On the one hand , nice, because these conflicts only stand in the way of our happiness; on the other hand, lousy, because we don't want to take any chances by having you visit me. Ina, we must indeed try to do it this way, although it isn't easy. Once I am up again, we will take care of it in the same beautiful way as before. Now Manja is coming here again soon, so for Heaven's sake, let's not take any chances. She is positively capable of telling your papa, and I think you too want to avoid that. Just in case an opportunity arises, I will send you a sign. Sweetheart, we have to, for God's sake, just get through these next two days. If there is no possibility for an occasion to visit, you will get, in any event, another little note from me.

Goodbye darling of mine,
I hold you in my thoughts,
your Jaap

P.S. Too tired to write more. I hope at least that you can read this.

———■　■———

Thursday, October 12, 1944

My dearest darling,

During roll call, a little chat with you. We are confronted here with our newest complication, for as you have already heard, Manja was released from the hospital and of course has a few days off now, which she plans to put to good use by visiting me often. I really have the impression that she is sorry about what happened, but despite that, I do not forget for a moment that her feelings about you haven't changed. In the meantime, she plops herself down in our little world again, with the new role of being the perfect wife. But my dear Ineke, know well that for Jaap there is only one "Number 1." If we both deal with the knowledge that these few days too will pass (I think Manja goes back to work on Monday), then the best that could happen would be that these few days will improve our archives, and in 26 years, when we are celebrating our 25th wedding anniversary, they will write and perform a great revue about our lives. Am I not an optimist? If you can make it, come around 2:00 P.M., this afternoon, a lousy time for you if you want to sleep; but it is probably safe then. I slept pretty well, although the sleeping pill didn't work for more than a couple of hours. I shaved this morning, but it was very painful due to the swelling. And you, sweet lady, can't even profit from it. Goodbye sweetheart, I hope I will see you this afternoon.

Many, many kisses,
your Jaap

Friday, October 13, 1944

My dearest Ineke,

This afternoon's visit worked out perfectly, because just as I thought, Manja came about 15 minutes after your departure, in a really good mood; so either she saw you and is at peace with it or, and this seems to me more logical, she didn't see you, meaning we escaped a big uproar. I feel sick again, but that sometimes happens.

You didn't look well at all this afternoon, and I am a little bit worried about it. Please darling, don't get sick. Even when we see each other so little, I do believe that these little glimpses of each other give us strength for the day.

Goodbye, lady of mine, sleep well.

Jaap

———■　■———

Saturday, October 14, 1944

My little dear lady,

How can I be mad at you, I love you too much for that; and besides, your decision is as sensible as it is upsetting. Of course we can't do it, and I understand completely if you tell me you cried after what happened this afternoon. It is as if we are doing things that are forbidden, which we must hide, even though everything is so good and pure between us. If you come to the wise conclusion that you'd rather not see me in this way, I can only say: I am so very happy that I have found in Ina a lovely as well as an understanding woman. Oh, darling, you don't know how terrible I felt this afternoon when I pushed you away. You, who I place as *number one* in my life, and then in the way that I did it! Yet it was still the best thing to do at that moment, and I think you also know that well. Tomorrow, more. It is so dark here that I am writing by the feel of the paper. Sleep well.

Many, many kisses, your Jaap

Sunday morning, October 15, 1944

My dearest Ineke,

7:00 A.M.–I had a very disturbing night. I didn't close my eyes at all because of the lice and also mainly because I itched all over, which is a side effect of my jaundice. I think that Manja will have to go back to work tomorrow. She is trying to get into the potato kitchen, but I doubt that she will succeed. I just got a note from Dr. van der Reiss indicating that I'm still positive. In any case, it keeps me free from work today. Now I am going to sleep some more. How are you? Do you still think about me a little bit? Goodbye darling, keep your spirits up, you hear?

Many, many kisses,

your Jaap

SEPARATION

Ina:

The Germans didn't want to set up a diamond factory anymore because it was beginning to seem unfeasible there, although all the machinery for such an undertaking was still available to them. We were kept in case the Germans won the war; they would still have two experts in the field who would assist them: my father and Mr. Asscher.

The workers in the diamond group were sent to Buchenwald, from where only three men returned, and the younger women were sent to the Beendorf salt mines, where horrible conditions existed, although more of them survived. The old women and children were transferred to the large women's camp next to the Sternlager, (Anne Frank's); and, miraculously, quite a few of the children survived.

168

Jaap and I were separated in February 1945, when the Asschers and our family were placed in a small separate compound in Bergen-Belsen, referred to as the Schneebaumlager, which derived its name from the Jewish elder there; and we were told that we would soon be transported to an internment camp in Switzerland. The plan however came to a halt in April, when the liberators were close to the camp, and the Germans decided to evacuate parts of Bergen-Belsen.

———■ ■———

*Monday afternoon, February 5, 1945

Dearest Jaapje,

A first bit of news from here. A complete nightmare! Last night with Josette in one bed on the boards without a mattress! The sanitation is indescribable: filthy, much worse than at yours! As to food, we will surely have an improvement. I hope it will quickly help our sick Uncle Hans, who has a fever and diarrhea. He had a temperature of 104° this morning. Of course we don't feel too happy. Maybe we will be. The worst part is: no little visits from you, which I miss very much. The saving grace of the day are the little stoves, which are wonderful when we have food. Now my darling, I am too depressed for anything nicer. Never say die. Goodbye for now! 1,000 kisses, Ina

*All Ina's letters that were saved were written from the Schneebaumlager compound. Jaap's letters, in response to these, were lost in Ina's rucksack on the day she was liberated except for two. A full account of this episode is included in the Editor's Notes.

Tuesday morning, February 6, 1945

Good morning, Sweetheart,

Still the same lot, with again, the same sleeping conditions. Waiting for the visit of *Lubbe*, in all probability today. Jaapje darling, I lost something very important, namely my notes with addresses, with among others, yours on it. Could you, when you have a chance, send me a separate letter with a few of your addresses on it? Just imagine if I couldn't find you again!! - Sweetheart, I hope that you feel somewhat more fit, and that today or tomorrow you can start again in full spirits. Give Manja my regards. Is she improving?

Much, much love, and a big hug from <u>Ina</u>. Bye, angel!

Lubbe was one of the higher ranking German SS officers, who had information of the Soep family's promised transport to Switzerland.

——— ■ ■ ———

Monday, February 19, 1945

My dearest Jaap,

Just a sign of life from this camp where they just leave us alone to rot like animals (excuse the expression!). Uncle Hans is lying on his deathbed, and a doctor still hasn't come. We hope that Lita will pull through, but there is nothing and no one to help ease his pain even a little bit. He is terribly congested, and he can't even turn himself over any more. You can understand that the mood here isn't all too gay. Above all, father is very much down and depressed, which is only logical. Aunt Leni has been very strong up till now, and so are the children. Oh darling, why is it all taking so very much too long? Every time you think that now it is almost over, then there are so many more victims; and even though it seems so scarily close, you begin to despair if it will ever come to an end.

I don't hear much good news from your camp either, only that there are still many deaths, right? But, my darling, I will try, as you have advised me, to be selfish and try to come through well myself. Shall we do our best to concentrate on that together? Give my regards to Manja. (How is she? Is her * *Love in Full Bloom?*) Juul, Freddy, Liesje, + children, and for you, much , much love and many kisses from your

Ina

* *This refers to a play on words based on the name of a famous Dutch Orators' Guild, from the 1700's, called "Blooming in Love."*

——■   ■——

Tuesday morning in haste

Dearest, yesterday afternoon at 6:00 P.M.. Uncle Hans died; age 43.

Ina:

We still knew nothing of the other camps. One day when I was still in the first camp in Bergen-Belsen, I saw a huge contingent of women through the barbed wire fence walking by in striped uniforms. I had never seen anyone in uniform at the camp because we wore our own clothing with the yellow stars. I recognized a young woman whom I knew and called out to her "Where are you coming from?" She answered, "We are coming from Auschwitz." Of course I knew of Auschwitz because people from Westerbork had been sent there. So I quickly asked, "Oh my God, where is so and so, and so and so?", friends I knew had been sent with her. She looked at me incredulously and said, "Don't you know?" I said, "Don't I know what?" She answered flatly, "Don't you know they were all gassed!" I was struck dumb. That was the first time that I heard anything like that. It was probably October 1944. When I went back and reported this to Jaap and my parents, no one could believe the concept of gas chambers. I told them, "They were probably told to tell us this in order to make us even more miserable than we are."

———— ■   ■ ————

Saturday, February 24, 1945

My sweet darling,

Yesterday we had a crazy and emotion-filled day. First, Uncle Hans' funeral. How terribly shameful it was, without a casket, with rough capos throwing the body on a cart—which was terrible for everybody, but especially for his wife and two children who are only 14 and 9 years old. And then a distraction came in the form of packages, one for Lisette, 2 for Leni, AND 3 for us. I am worried about my father; he has such a hard time. This afternoon the SS men came into the camp, with the result that it looks now as if this camp will not be our last; and it looks as if they had a plan for us which they could not finalize. It seems that this camp will be completely evacuated. The Turkish people are leaving soon. Probably the Spaniards as well. I am very anxious to know what is in store for us. We are trying for possibilities such as Theresienstadt, (with special treatment), and Liebenau. I wish that we already knew. Jaapje darling, the news from your camp is getting worse by the day, soon there will be nothing left. I shudder to talk to anyone who comes......

Your Ina

Ina:

Of course they didn't have funerals in Bergen-Belsen, but I guess I didn't know what else to call it, with us following behind the Germans when they threw my uncle's body on the cart.

———■　■———

Monday morning, March 5, 1945

My dearest love,

"Sag beim abschied leise servus,"; ("When you depart, quietly say goodbye,") (from the song by the Viennese chanteuse, *GRETA KELLER*). Yes, my Jaap, now it is actually coming. Exactly when, we don't know yet. People say that we first must be deloused, and that the machine for it still has to be repaired, otherwise we would have left earlier. Furthermore, there is a diphtheria case in our group, and a scarlet fever case, which is quite a scary thing; but I don't think it will hold us up. People say that we are going to *Liebenau, and some say via that camp free to go and live in Switzerland, but nobody knows exactly.

At the moment, it is a strange situation here. We are eating every bit of the small supplies that we still have, but if it takes too long, we will have nothing left to eat. The camp is dead quiet now that the Turks have left. We will leave with the Spaniards and Argentinians, and only approximately 12 Aryan women will stay behind. What is going to happen with the 90 South Americans?

*Liebenau was an internment camp for inmates with foreign nationalities on the Lake of Konstanz in Switzerland.

Dearest boy, now I am really going to take my leave, thus I will end this letter, because I don't know how to say goodbye. We know it all and that is enough!!

Much, much love, good kisses, etc.

Your Ina

P.S. Thank you very much for your letter. I was very happy with it! P.S. 2 - Just got your letter from Jacques. I was not pleased with its tone. Sweetheart, in God's name take care of yourself so I don't have to worry about you. I want to see you again in good health. The transport will still be another 4 or 5 days away. Dearest sweetheart, my thoughts are always with you. Kisses, Ina.

Ina:

In February 1944, my father had received a document in Westerbork that stated that we were citizens of El Salvador, signed by one of the unsung heroes of the European rescue effort. He was born George Mandel, a Romanian Jew, who was an honorary consul of El Salvador in Bucharest before the war, and who fled from the Nazis to Switzerland, where he occupied the same position in Geneva, changing his name to Mantello. With the consent of the Salvadoran government, he used his influence to grant Salvadoran citizenship papers to many European Jews, mostly to the Dutch and Belgians at first. Later many, many thousands more were given to the Hungarians without any charge. It gave my family immediate protection, since the Germans, somehow, honored citizenship in foreign countries, especially those that were not at war with them. I believe that this special protection afforded by this document was the most important factor in saving my family's lives, besides my father's prominence in the diamond industry.

———■　■———

Tuesday morning, March 13, 1945, 8:00 A.M.

My dearest boy,

It is getting more difficult to keep in contact, but maybe today I will somehow find a way. People are saying that we will have a quarantine bath tomorrow, and then on Thursday or Friday–the transport. God, let it be true! Did you also hear that by the end of the week the last of the people from Westerbork are expected in your camp? What a slap in the face they will get! Thankfully, Mother has almost completely perked up with some *Cibazol* tablets. Yesterday Josette, Joop, and I went to the dentist in the Women's Lager. It is so vast! It looks as if all the women of the world have gathered there. We saw a few people from our old group, but didn't have much of a chance to talk to them. It's great that you get to exercise your mind a little bit with your downstairs neighbor. It matters on these long days, and Jewish thought is so good as a distraction; in addition to the fact that it gives a true feeling of having a definite direction in your life. (It gives you a certain power and optimism.) I really hope that I will hear from you before our departure, also that this might very well be the last letter. Are you still so optimistic?–There is every reason for it! Sweetheart, I don't want to say goodbye again to you. Just, "see you soon!" I embrace and kiss you.

your Ina

Cibazol was an anti-diarrhea pill.

Ina:

One day I had a terrible toothache. It was common knowledge that there was a Polish woman dentist in the huge women's camp. So I was brought there to see if she could help me. That's when I saw the bodies- bodies- corpses! It was surrealistic!– unbelievable. They were either piled high on carts with women pulling them someplace, or stacked on the sides of the barracks. I shook involuntarily, and wanted to run out, screaming. But I controlled myself for the sake of those women who had to live there. Many of those mass deaths had occurred because the people who had been shipped out of Auschwitz were already at death's door. So they died very soon here. And in this huge women's camp, the food situation was many times worse than in our small camp. They died in such large numbers every day so rapidly that they could not clear the bodies out fast enough. Alive, barely alive and dead, they all stayed together.

———■ ■———

Friday, March 16, 1945, 12:30 P.M.

My sweet darling,

No one knows anything more about our departure, although the rumor is that we are going. I suspect that the problem with our not leaving is that there is no train available. This afternoon we will be vaccinated against typhus. The optimists say that it is in connection with the transport; the pessimists say that spotted typhus is breaking out in all the camps. And what do we do? We just wait and see! Jaapje dear, I share your hunger problems, yes! We are being very naughty with our bread. The food sometimes comes at 4:00 P.M. in the afternoon, and sometimes early in the morning, and we are all complaining a lot. We just heard that from now on we will get evening soup only twice a week. Go ahead, we won't notice a little more or a little less hunger! The small stock of food we had is totally gone, but at least we ate well for a week. How are things with Dr. A? I heard that it is not what they were afraid of. Can Manja go and be with him, and does she also take care of you a little? Sweetheart, will this be the last letter? Will you help me make it true? I really have no more patience! For you much love, kisses and anything you want from your Ina.

5:00 P.M.

Just got your letter. Very happy with it! Great that you are so much better. If you feel well enough, you should start working again, in view of the 4 extra food portions. The men just had to go suddenly to the quarantine bath. We go later or tomorrow. It looks as if the transport will leave soon. Bye, dearest. Heartfelt kisses, Ina.

Ina:

People stole food. The hungrier people became, the more they stole. I suffered a great deal from what was termed "camp sickness", but it was actually typhoid fever with the accompanying very high fever for 3 or 4 days, and terrible intestinal upsets. I couldn't eat a thing. My sister would save my daily ration of bread meant to last from breakfast through supper. Once, when she went to look for it, it had been stolen. When this happened, Manja was the first one to offer some of her own bread ration. People who were desperate enough weren't kind or decent anymore. We saw the most honorable people we knew from Amsterdam descend to very low levels of morality when they were starving, and were forced to think of nothing but their own self-preservation. But none of these people survived. There was that last-ditch effort to stay alive for a few days, and then they would be gone. It was heart-rending to watch people deteriorate before your eyes, especially the men, who seemed to have a harder time in sustaining themselves than the women–mentally, as well as physically. It was numbing having to endure worse and worse overcrowding with rampant disease, complete lack of sanitary facilities, and pitifully meager food rations. But this was our situation.

———■　■———

THIS IS "THE TRAIN" IN WHICH INA AND HER FAMILY RODE OUT FROM BERGEN-BELSEN FOR SIX DAYS AND SIX NIGHTS WITH 2400 PEOPLE WHO WERE LIBERATED BY THE AMERICAN 9TH ARMY ON FRIDAY, APRIL 13, 1945. THIS IS THE EXACT SCENE THE LIBERATORS SAW AT FIRST GLANCE. THE SOEP FAMILY WAS COOKING IN THE AREA WHERE THE SMOKE IS COMING FROM. THE PHOTO WAS TAKEN BY ONE OF THE SOLDIERS, AND, WEEKS LATER, WAS BOUGHT BY A YOUNG FELLOW SURVIVOR FROM THE ASSCHER GROUP AT A KIOSK IN BRUSSELS WHERE WAR PIC-TURES WERE BEING SOLD FROM HANGING CLIPS. HE HAD GONE TO THE CITY TO FIND HIS MOTHER WHO HAD BEEN IN HIDING THERE, AND RETURNED WITH FIVE PICTURES, ONE OF WHICH ("THE TRAIN") HE OFFERED TO INA.

INA HAS BEEN CARRYING THIS PHOTOGRAPH IN HER WALLET FOR 55 YEARS WHICH ACCOUNTS FOR IT'S BATTERED CONDI-TION NOW. IT IS LIKE A TALISMAN FOR HER.

THE OFFICIAL WEDDING PORTRAIT. JANUARY 29, 1946.

INA AND JAAP POLAK ON THEIR WEDDING DAY,
JANUARY 29, 1946.

THE WEDDING PARTY WITH THE BRIDE AND GROOM IN THE CENTER.

ON VACATION IN SCHEVENINGEN, A NORTH SEA COASTAL TOWN NEAR
THE HAGUE, INA IS EXPECTING THE COUPLE'S FIRST CHILD, 1946.

WITH THE FIRST-BORN SON, FREDERICK BENNO,
ARRIVED NOVEMBER 8, 1946.

A SECOND SON, ANTHONY GERALD WAS BORN
ON MARCH 4, 1949.

ON THE BOAT TO AMERICA, 1951.

MARGRIT BETTY POLAK WAS BORN NOVEMBER 17, 1955.

GROWING UP IN EASTCHESTER, NEW YORK, 1960.

JAAP POLAK WITH HIS TWO SISTERS, BETTY AND LIESJE, AT
HIS EIGHTY-FIFTH BIRTHDAY PARTY, JANUARY 2, 1998.

DAUGHTER MARGRIT, INA, AND INA'S MOTHER, TONI SOEP, ON HER
EIGHTIETH BIRTHDAY, DECEMBER 8, 1975, AT THE POLAK HOME.

THE POLAK FAMILY ON THE OCCASION OF JAAP'S KNIGHTHOOD BESTOWED BY QUEEN BEATRIX OF T
NETHERLANDS AT THE DUTCH CONSULATE ON JAAP'S EIGHTIETH BIRTHDAY, DECEMBER 31, 1992.
TOP ROW, FROM LEFT, ANTHONY GERALD POLAK, HARVEY SHIELD, SOFIA BETTINA SHIELD, INA AND JA
POLAK, FREDERICK BENNO POLAK.
BOTTOM ROW FROM LEFT, JAMIE MOSS POLAK, AMY MOSS POLAK, EMILY LAUREN POLAK, MARGI
BETTY POLAK SHIELD, ANN ELYSE POLAK, CARRIE SILLS POLAK, JOSHUA ANDREW POLAK.

PHOTO TAKEN BY ROBERT PREST

THE POLAK FAMILY CELEBRATING JAAP'S EIGHTY-FIFTH BIRTHDAY AND INA'S SEVENTY-FIFTH BIRTHDAY
THE CARLYLE HOTEL IN NEW YORK CITY ON JANUARY 2, 1998.
STANDING FROM LEFT, CARRIE, JOSHUA, ANN, FRED, MARGRIT, HARVEY, AMY, TONY, EMILY, JAMIE.
SEATED, INA, SOFIA AND JAAP.

PHOTO TAKEN BY LESLIE I

Sabbath, March 17, 1945, 12:30 P.M.

My dear, dear little Jaap,

This morning I received two letters from you. I really enjoyed your sermons. They were so wonderful, and different from camp life. Except for your food stories, which I found offensive. We were all very angry that you talked about chicken noodle soup, when all we get are groats and turnips! I can tell from the tone of your letter that you are still quite strong, and that you make the best of our pathetic life here, and that gives me such unbelievable pleasure. That is the most important strength for our race to the finish line!

Last night, we women had a one hour quarantine bath. "All blankets and clothes that you own must go into the truck to be deloused...." This morning I found my last two house-lice dead in my sweater. I can't tell you how lucky I feel to be rid of them. But for how long? We sleep underneath Bill, who has the top bunk, and we don't know how much longer he'll be sick. And we know nothing about this sudden quarantine bath in relationship to our transport. We have heard nothing, but we have hopes of leaving tomorrow or the next day. My darling boy, I am going to do something very important. Eat! We had a surprise today, a beet soup, but with potatoes and bread! We are old and decrepit, and so hungry that my sense of humor is dying. Maybe I'll write more this afternoon. (In English). So long, dearest!

2:00 P.M.

Hello! I ate so well! It is true that I had no utensils, and it wasn't cut up, but you must make do with what you have. With this letter my dear, I am also thinking so much about our coming home, and besides the fact that I am sure it will be great, I do stop to ask questions. Where, when will we find each other again? If at all, we may be, in reality, returning to The Netherlands. However, in all probability, we might find it easier to go to America. And, if I go there with my family, how will our feelings withstand this distance?

Above all, what will we do if you are not liberated at the same time as we are? Oh, my young man, everything is so vague.

———■　■———

Monday morning, March 19, 1945, 8:30 A.M.
My always dearest Ineke,

I have the feeling that this is truly one of my last letters and I only hope that it reaches you. I was very happy with your two letters. There is also a good mood in the camp now because either today or tomorrow everyone will get a package from Sweden: each is supposed to have one lb. of butter, 1 kilogram of sugar, crackers, and powdered milk. How do you like that? I still can't believe it, and have to see it first. In the meantime, this morning I gave myself an advance of some extra bread. To receive something like this is terribly important for the whole camp, as it could mean our rescue. I didn't have a fever yesterday, but last night I had diarrhea for the first time in three weeks, although I'm sure it will pass. We had exceptionally good food yesterday: white cabbage with a lot of potatoes, remarkably tasty and good. The food has been significantly better in the last 3 days. They say that there is a new commission in the kitchen. There is a chance that I will receive extra food fairly regularly now via B. As long as that is possible, I will not try to force my way out of here, and wait until they make me leave. With double food and rest, it is best to stick it out here. In your Shabbat letter, you asked another question which I have thought about a lot. It is indeed not out of the question that you will go to America via Switzerland before the end of the war; and Ineke, if you do end up there, I am beginning to despair. However, that may be nonsensical. After the war, I think we will find that the distance which beforehand seemed beyond reach, will seem smaller and not as difficult to bridge. I strongly believe that I will end up in The Netherlands, possibly making use of my connections with B. And the most important thing

180

then, is that Manja will want us to have a very quick divorce, so on this subject I hope for more good possibilities than difficulties. In the worst case, you will be in America and I will be in Amsterdam. I must tell you then, quite honestly, that a lot will then depend on your feelings. You know my feelings. I am not so easily discarded. I will need a lot of time to build up a business, and I have the feeling that I will be walking around Amsterdam with the sense that my one and only love lives in New York. For you, it will be completely different. Not that I doubt your feelings for even one moment, sweet darling. But you would be coming to America as a lovely young girl after two years of camp life into a society that will receive you with open arms, and which will offer you everything you could want. And even though you wouldn't forget about me, I have an idea that you will meet men who are more interesting, who are better company, more charming, and better in these capacities than I am. And if our chances for personal contact are then limited to letter writing, which is very nice, but not conducive to the creation of a marriage, I really believe that everything that we have built up will go no further. My dear little lady, these are my pessimistic thoughts now, based on the worst possible situation that could occur. In between, there are so many better solutions that are possible; for instance, you in America, but coming back with your father for a few months; and then I, via my Bram Van Dam contacts perhaps, or Gitters' in South America, coming to America, which attracts me just as much as Holland. Even though it will be much more difficult to build up a career there, I could then offer you everything, because I want so much to offer you everything. So the best thing would be you and I in Amsterdam, where we could then thoroughly contemplate our future plans for relocating. But as much as we think about it, you are right when you say that everything will be as it must be, and in these things, I have a true faith in God. If I review in my thoughts how Our Good Lord has protected us both, as individuals and together, then we must look into the future with faith. For you, I think of the fearful days when you were in Westerbork's hospital and put on the transport list to Auschwitz; and furthermore, how you could live through camp life with an illness like asthma which is totally unsuited to this way of life. As for myself, there were so many times in Westerbork when I was on the verge of being put on transport, then I tried to go to Theresienstadt, then later I tried the "1,000 list", (which in the end meant going to Auschwitz), that it must have been God's protection which brought me here together with you. In Westerbork, we had an ever improving relationship until Manja spoiled it all; and then when I was here, I realized how much I missed you; and then you came here, and Manja also tried to change things here. Finally, there was my kitchen period here which was very important for both of our stomachs, although I wish I could have filled your stomach even better. So darling, a little recapitulation of all that we have gone through, and I still think with such great pleasure about all the wonderful things which will be carried into the future, strengthened by the sure feeling that Our Good Lord will offer us the chupah.* And now, sweetest, just a little more talk, and then done with this letter, which has become a true farewell letter.

So I end, goodbye dearest sweetheart of mine, stay as you are, then you will stay mine. In thoughts, many kisses, your Jaap

P.S. In the meantime our package arrived. One for each! 1 pound of butter, 12 crackers, 1 kilogram of sugar, 2 bouillon cubes, and 1 package of pea meal. It is really terrific, and really needed. So I will eat my crackers tomorrow. In any case no one will be hungry for one week.

*The Chupah is the traditional arbor, or covering beneath which Jewish couples are married.

Jaap:

There was a new set of bosses in the kitchen at this time, which accounted for the improvements.

Bram van Dam was my boss in the Carlton Hotel in Amsterdam before the war. He was a wonderful man from whom I learned a lot about the hotel business in the years 1930-1933. He survived the war in hiding. Ina's father, Abraham Soep, and he were good friends, and I would feel very proud to give his name as reference when I asked for Ina's hand in marriage. I thought that perhaps Ina's father would be sending Ina to America to try to counteract her involvement with me if he did not approve of me as a suitor. My father-in-law had already established prior business interests in America as early as the 1930's.

——■　■——

Tuesday morning, March 20, 1945, 10:30 A.M.

My always dearest love,

Heartfelt thanks for your fine letter from yesterday. I cannot tell you how happy I am about the tone in which you express yourself. I'll tell you honestly that I was made to feel very uneasy in the beginning of your sickness by your mental state, and that means that I am glad that we didn't go away then. If we leave now, I will go with peace in my heart. People say that we will leave this week, as the group which we are waiting for to be exchanged with is waiting in Switzerland, but this sounds to me like an IPA.... This morning we went into the forest twice to gather wood. It was fantastic, as if you were walking in *Blaricum*! For a moment you knew what it was like to be a free person in the open air. I know I will quickly grow accustomed to that!! It was great to read your contemplations on the future, and I also have much hope and confidence that we will find each other wherever we may land, led by our feelings and Our Good Lord who has been so good to us up till now.–Our sick people are improving. I suspect that you will be going to a disinfection bath one of these days. At the moment, only the Hungarians are going. If it is at all possible, go with them. You would pass close to our fence, and that would be a real opportunity for us to talk for a moment.

Dear little darling of mine, I finish this last letter (for the how "many'th" time ?) I fervently hope that I will see your darling mug once more before we leave, and otherwise until....?

Stay as strong, stalwart, and buoyant as you are now, and everything will turn out well!

Love and kisses, and in my innermost thoughts, your Ina.

*Blaricum is a suburb of Amsterdam at the edge of a woodsy area.

———■　■———

Tuesday, March 27, 1945, 8:45 A.M.

My dearest boy,

Yesterday was extremely agitating: Meurs was here! He really brought very little news, spoke a lot about transport difficulties, and gave a departure date of anywhere from two days to four weeks. He told us that three weeks ago he had waited three days for us at the place of destination. He talked about a camp which used to be "filthy," where he had new barracks built for us, with small rooms, running water, shower stalls, etc. He mentioned theatre, movies, <u>no barbed wire</u>, and special care for the children. All in all it sounds, a lot like Theresienstadt with special treatment. Indeed, when Father asked him if we are going to the *Bodensee, he answered: "So weit ist es nicht," ("We aren't that far yet.") Going to a neutral country is out of the question. It was really a big disappointment for all of us, but as I say, it's our own fault for letting ourselves believe all the IPAs. Has he come to you, and what have the discussions been about during the last few days?—My young darling, will I hear from you soon? How your work is going, the food, your new abode, etc. I stop now until the next time–when that will be I do not know, because I also have letter-transport difficulties here; but we will soon find somebody.

*Bodensee is a lake in Switzerland where the Soeps had been told they would be sent.

———■ ■———

Monday, April 2, 1945, 2:00 P.M.

My dearest Ineke,

This time it has been a while since you've heard from me. First of all, it is due to delivery difficulties, which we hope have now been overcome. In any event, confirm that you received this letter so that I know that it got into the right hands. It doesn't look as if you will be leaving; and if we were soon to have a quick departure together from here, we just don't know about it. Although I still can't believe that it will be only one or two weeks, I also believe that we will not have to live in this misery much longer. Everything points to the end being near, so grit your teeth! First of all, the situation here. Fortunately, the spotted typhus is mild here. It's not spreading too much, so there is no reason for anxiety. There have been *only* two deaths, both men who were working outside the camp. Furthermore, no one has come into the camp. There is a lot of barbed wire and fencing around the offices and the Albanian barracks, but that is not important. We have not had a roll call in three weeks. They undoubtedly have other worries. The food service here is very difficult due to the unbelievably crazy hours that the food arrives. This week we had to go to bed between 10 and 11:00 P.M. at night, and then up again in the morning for coffee at about 4:30. Of course I compensate for that by sleeping during the day, but I stay tired. On the other hand, and this is the most important thing, the food is excellent in both quality and quantity: about 3-4 liters of soup, and I don't have the terrible hunger that I had before. People have asked me to be the Barrack Leader of Barrack 33, a big honor; but after a lot of discussion, I refused, because the <u>official</u> food advantages are practically nil, and I wouldn't think of accepting more than what is officially allowed. Also Manja's friend B. advised me to stay where I am. Last night, we got 10 extra cigarettes and I hope we will have more extras like that. The relationship with Manja has become somewhat better. Once again she is friendly. It is better this way than the other way around. Dr. A. is nearly recovered, but due to the stricter conditions she sees very little of him, and he will probably have to go back to the hospital very soon. How wonderful that you had a nice Seder! I was hauling food barrels at the time, but was eventually able to go to the Seder at the nursing home barrack. It sounds crazy, dearest girl, but there are days in which I have absolutely no time to write. But for today, make do with this little story about the camp and me, and in a few days I will write more. Who knows, if I believe all the optimistic news here, maybe in a few days........

Bye, sweetheart. Regards to all. I kiss you and embrace you. your Jaap.

Jaap:

Even though I was flattered to be offered such a prominent and prestigious position as Barrack Leader, I somehow felt it was important not to accept it. You were at all times held accountable for the number of people there; and the Germans might come in at any time to blame the Barrack Leader for whatever infraction they could make up.

As the Germans realized the end was drawing near, food quality and quantity improved considerably, (but not for everyone), because they were depleting their supplies. This was one week before departure.

Ina:

The Seder, the meal celebrating Passover, the Jewish holiday commemorating liberation from Egyptian bondage, was especially poignant for us in the camp, for we felt we were again in bondage. We tried to get all the traditional symbols for food on the table anyhow. We used grass for parsley, and we needed an egg, so I said, "I have an egg," and I brought out my wooden darning "egg" I used for mending socks. I will always keep that "egg" in my sewing kit. It made me recall with sadness the beautiful Seders we used to have at home with the white damask tablecloths, and a big Seder dish, two-tiered, with little curtains in front of it, and the usual symbolic ingredients behind it.

———■   ■———

Saturday morning, April 7, 1945

My dearest Jaap,

Last night at 8:00 P.M., we were called for transport, and had to be ready in two hours; but we are still here. No idea where to; only hoping that it is good. Don't have anything else to say: hope to see you again very soon.

We received your latest news. We have enough bread, butter and sugar for approximately four days for all of us, so no problem with that. Maybe we will get more from here also. Send special regards to Carla, Freddy, Juul, Liesje, Manja, and everyone else. For you, all the love and good things that you wish for, I am, your Ina.

LIBERATION:INA SOEP

Ina: April, 1945

The day of liberation for me was Friday, April 13, 1945, by members of the American 9th Army. The first news item we heard came from the soldiers, which saddened us all: the death of President Franklin Roosevelt the day before.

We had been sent out on a passenger train with freight cars in the rear where people who were unable to sit up were lying on the floors. We could sit, but we could never lie down. We rode for six days and six nights, riding for an hour, stopping for a half hour, riding for an hour, stopping for two hours, never knowing why or what for. Apparently, the engineer was waiting for orders from Berlin; and finally, at what turned out to be our last stop, a top SS official came, and what I found out later was that he ordered the engineer to drive the whole train into the Elbe River. Some Hungarian prisoners, who'd come into Bergen-Belsen rather late into the war, (end of 1944), and had smuggled in a lot of gold sewn into their clothing, learned of the decision, and bribed the engineer with their gold to stay exactly where we were. He agreed, because he knew that the war was almost over; and that he might get some kind of reprieve for saving lives. The next day, the official came back, furious, wanting to know why his orders had not been carried out, and said he would return that afternoon and did not want to see that train again.

We were allowed to go into the nearby village and ask for food. We got some potatoes and an egg. We were so happy to see ONE egg; and I remember our family sharing it. We had a feeling that this was really the end, because we heard shooting and bombing from not too far away. We made a little fire, and were sitting there next to the train, cooking potatoes when, all of a sudden, these big, uniformed soldiers came over the hill and down into the valley where the train had stopped, with their rifles in shooting position, because they had no idea what or who they were running into. I remember seeing them smiling, with perfect white teeth, and thinking they must have all been to the same orthodontist. When they reached us, they found this long train with 2,400 people in it; and when they found out who we were and what we were all about, they informed us of our liberation. We were FREE!!

As the soldiers surrounded us, I was overcome with the strangest feelings. Liberation!!!! After years in the camps, we were free—freed from being captive any longer. How does one act after years under guard–being told what to do and when to do it, always with the threat of punishment or worse. What would happen now? What about Jaap?–and Rudi? So many other questions crowded my mind. I was overjoyed at the prospect of going home; and yet as we sat on the dirt in the small hill above the railroad tracks, looking down at the train in the middle of Germany, I could hear the moans and the crying of the ill and dying coming from the rear freight cars. It was a combination of extreme emotions that I will always remember of that memorable day.

The people of the nearest village, Farsleben, were forced to take us in, and we stayed with a farm family who made us bacon and eggs. After dinner, Josette and I found more food set out in barrels in the streets. We got very sick that night, because our stomachs could not digest fatty foods any more. Many people died after liberation because of this, but we didn't know any better at that time. The next morning, the Americans came and told us that we had to evacuate, because the village was in danger of being recaptured by the Germans. Later, we learned that the real reason was to isolate our group to prevent the spread of typhus infection to the German civilian population.

It was that morning, when it was raining so hard, that the bottom of my rucksack, which had served me so well for nineteen months, fell out, and I lost all my letters to Jaap which I had stored in the bottom. They fell into a huge puddle where I reluctantly left them.

We had different kinds of experiences in the following days. The night of my father's birthday, while we were living in the villa of the German SS Commander of the abandoned military village, Hillersleben, we served a fine birthday dinner, with the canned goods from the basement, on the table in the large dining room with elegant china, crystal, silver, and linen, all with his initials on them. The Commander happened to have the same initials as my father: A.S. After almost three weeks, we spent our last night in Germany in an assembly hall, waiting for repatriation to Holland the next morning, when we

191

were awakened from our sleep well before dawn, and rushed outside with our meager belongings, as we watched the wooden structure burning to the ground. We watched big wooden cut-outs of the heads of Hitler, Goering, and Goebbels that were attached to the roof of the building tumble down in the fire as we cheered.

My parents had to stay back in Germany, as my father fell gravely ill with spotted typhus. They were repatriated about one month later, after his recovery Western Holland was liberated from the German occupation on May 5, 1945, the same day my sister and I arrived in Eindhoven in the Southeast part of Holland, which had been free since September 1944.

Conditions in the newly liberated West, where Amsterdam is located, were so bad after the cruel *hunger winter*, that it took several weeks before anybody was able to go there. The roads were not passable, and there was not enough food. Kind people in Eindhoven took the new repatriates into their own homes until they could go back to their own towns and cities in the West.

In Amsterdam, I was taken in by the family of one of my best friends, the van Santens, who had survived by hiding; my sister, by other friends who were gentile.

LIBERATION : JAAP POLAK

As time wore on, conditions at the camp went from bad to worse and worse, until they became unbearable. You did not die at once. It was a slow fading away—slow, because after all, it was a *privileged* camp.

We knew that the war would be over soon, and with the camp increasingly becoming a stinking hole of mud, cruelty, hunger, disease, and hundreds of deaths each day, we did not know if we should hope to be taken away to an unknown place, or wait for liberation.

On April 9th, it was finally our turn. Two days earlier, 2,400 inmates had already left–Ina's train.

We did not know how badly the war was going for the Germans, so we thought we might even be transferred to another camp. We knew only that the British army was near Bergen-Belsen, but we had heard this sort of rumor before.

The cattle cars waiting for us had brought in inmates from other camps; the newcomers were in even worse physical state than we: two struggling drawn-out columns of walking skeletons passed each other on the road, and the station was five miles from the camp. But we were still *privileged*. When we arrived at the train, only fifty prisoners were put in each box car. That number was normally much higher. The difference meant that we were able–with difficulty–to sit on the floor, taking turns to stretch out. I remember that we had a water pail and a latrine bucket in each of two corners of the car.

And then the train started to roll, and we had no idea where we were headed. Each morning we stopped, and the people who had died on the train had to be carried out and buried. I was one of the people who had to do this since I was in better shape than most; and during that two-week train ride, I buried many of my friends in graves we dug at the places where we stopped. We lost an unbelievable number of people on that train.

We passed Hamburg, we passed Berlin, but still proceeded very slowly because of clogged railroad nets, lack of fuel, and worn out equipment. The miserable, interminable journey finally came to an end on April 23 in Troebitz, a village 35 miles from Leipzig, where at 6 a.m. in the morning, Russian troops approached the train, and suddenly, we were FREE!!!! That first day, I went with a group of other survivors to get food by going to farmers' homes; and I remember that we got a cow, which one of the boys at the farm said he would kill for us. I went back to the village, felt suddenly weak, and fainted. That day, I succumbed to the horrible illness, spotted typhus, no doubt contracted from burying the typhus victims all during the train ride. I was placed in a private home, stayed in a coma for two days until April 25; then, delirious with terrible hallucinations and thirsty all the time, I was bedridden for a week. When I finally recovered, I weighed seventy pounds. But.... I HAD SURVIVED THE HOLOCAUST!!!!!

For two months we stayed in Troebitz; and gradually, the disease receded. Our main concern then was that we were going to be sent to Russia, since our communication with the Russians was so minimal that we heard nothing, and assumed the worst. But finally, the repatriation came.

One bright morning–unannounced–a long column of American trucks lined up in the village street, and we were told to be ready in a hurry. We left behind three hundred and fifty people, who had died in Troebitz after our liberation. One was my sister Juul, who died on the same day I came out of my coma, two days after the liberation. Then we were taken from East Germany to Frankfurt in West Germany. We remained in Frankfurt just a few days, and were then flown to Maastricht in Holland. There we immediately had medical examinations, and in my case, they found that I suffered from pleurisy, which required that I be under observation for three months. My sister, Betty, came to visit me, and it was only then that I learned what she and her husband had done in the Resistance. Her husband was caught and tried and executed by the Germans for blowing up a train.

Finally, I returned to Amsterdam, with a front tooth missing, complete loss of hair, (a side effect of typhus), wearing Red Cross supplied clothing and shoes. At our first meeting, one of my friends kiddingly remarked, "You were never handsome, but look at you now!" My weight at that point was already up to 110 pounds; and I only hoped that Ina could accept me the way I looked at that moment.

195

I found a room in Amsterdam–which was difficult with the prevailing housing shortage–and I also helped Manja find a place of her own. Thus, we split immediately; and I made the necessary arrangements to obtain a *Geth*, the Orthodox divorce document. The religious ceremony that accompanies this marriage dissolution took place in August, 1945.

———■   ■———

(From Ina) Eindhoven, Holland, May 13, 1945
Dear Pops and Moms,

How are things with you? I'm sure not as good as with us. We are living here in the house of Bram and Elly de Jong. He is the president of the *J(ewish) C(oordination) C(ommission)*. It is as if we never left Holland. The train trip, which to our great surprise, took us straight to Holland was very tiring but not unpleasant. We rode for three days and three nights in open wagons with people who helped us tremendously in every way. It was glorious weather, so that we all got dark suntans. Even at night, there wasn't a moment that we were cold. Lisette, Marianne, and Chelly rode in a covered car which was available only for a few of the very sick. In Maastricht, they went straight to the hospital. We then rode on to Eindhoven, and after two days at the War Repatriation Center, first in a warehouse, and then in a school, for delousing, registration, and medical examination, Bram de Jong gave us immediate housing. Tonight, Josette and I are going to our new address which is Douma,

* *The Jewish Coordination Commission was an organization that helped re-orient Jews returning to Holland.*

196

Wilgenroosstraat 48, Eindhoven. We have come across many people here who were in hiding. We just heard that 800 people are coming from Theresientadt to Holland, and among them is Professor Meyers. We are beginning to have contact with the west of Holland.

Dear ones, I am stopping, and hope that I will see you very soon, with the firm conviction that Father will have completely regained his health by then.

Bye; and many, many kisses,
your Ina.

Ina:

As new arrivals, my sister and I received extra food-ration coupons which helped the landlady, a young newlywed in planning and preparing meals. Food remained scarce at that time. Josette and I slept on the floor in a small spare room of the tiny apartment, on mattresses distributed by the Red Cross. Though it was all very skimpy and primitive, it was pure luxury compared to what we had suffered through.

———■ ■———

Wednesday evening, June 9, 1945, 8:00 P.M.

My dearest Ineke,

After an emotional trip–at 2:00 P.M. yesterday, we still didn't know that we were leaving–by truck from Troebitz near Dresden to Halle, where we arrived at midnight, and this morning by airplane to Holland. Home at last! No, not home; that will only be in Amsterdam. How happy I was to hear that all of you were alive, you can well imagine. Before anything else Ina, <u>everything is still as it was before; I hope it is with you too.</u> I hope that we will soon talk about everything in peace, (how I long for that, at last)! Manja is the same as ever. Our arrangement, however, is very well set up; and from her side, I am <u>sure</u>, there will be no more difficulties. Of course, things are off with her boyfriend; that also turned out to be nothing. Ineke, Our Good Lord is with us, in this case especially with me. Our whole transport suffered a very bad spotted typhus epidemic after we left. I myself was on the verge of death for two days, but pulled through! The same with Manja. After six weeks of being in a hospital in the forest with decent nourishment, (even more than others, as in the last few weeks I was allowed to help in the kitchen!), I am better, and I now look, although a shadow of what I once was, much better. I lost all my hair, but it is beginning to grow again nicely. Now about those who became victims of typhus and malnourishment! A sad list, including thirty good friends and relatives. What we went through after our transport out of Bergen-Belsen cannot be described. The most important things you know now. Tomorrow I will write more! Bye, darling of mine.

See you very, very soon.

In my thoughts I embrace you and kiss you, Jaap

P.S. The mail takes 5 days to get to you. But in case it takes longer, please write as soon as you can when you hear from me.

Herman Gorterstraat, Amsterdam
Monday, June 11, 1945, 2:00 P.M.

My dearest Jaap,

I can find no words to express how happy and thankful I am that you are at a reachable distance from me. I was beginning to panic a little, that I still hadn't heard anything, as information about several others began to trickle in. I am very excited and nervous, and almost can't wait to see you in real life and be able to embrace you—when the outsiders will let us do so! We all feel so terribly sad about the dreadful numbers of those who died. Oh my boy, how appalling. But then, I am doubly thankful that you pulled through. Our Good Lord, who for so long held His hand over our heads, once again did not abandon our ship. My dear little Jaap, we must talk about everything very carefully, and do nothing in haste, and must first learn to know each other well in a normal society. Oh sweetheart, there is such a crazy amount to tell you, and even more to ask you, but better orally, as this letter has to be sent off right away; someone is taking it with him. I am living with my best girlfriend, Wiesje van Santen. Do you already know where you are going to live? I will be staying here till we can go back into our own house, but may leave sooner. They are wonderful to me here, and I am free as a bird in the sky. I just can't believe my luck. Now that the uncertainty about you is also taken away, everything looks perfect although in the community there is still a lot missing, as you will see. But let's be selfish, and enjoy our own happiness, shouldn't we? How is Manja? Give her my regards, don't forget! And what are your immediate plans?–Did you know anything about us? Or were you as uncertain as we were about you?–How is Freddy doing? Is he very overwhelmed? My condolences to you and also to him with the loss of Juul which is doubly tragic, because the liberation was so close. So she made it through the whole wretched time for nothing.–

Darling, don't be startled when you see me, but I look healthier and stronger than I ever even looked before the war. I am physically almost recovered, and mentally as well. I tire very quickly, and need a lot of sleep, and find that every once in a while I still have a little strange and drowsy feeling in my head, but that will pass. Josette is even fatter than I am.

Dear sweetheart of mine, will I really see you very soon? Many regards for Manja, Freddy, and all the ones I know. For you, all that you want, and a bunch of kisses from your Ina.

Ina:

Wiesje van Santen worked in the Resistance for three years until caught by the Gestapo, who, during six months in solitary confinement, beat her badly. When she pretended cooperation, a very high official, her interrogator, fell in love with her and placed her in a house with high military officers. After five days, she fled. Now a danger to others, she hid at different addresses. Her back, injured in prison, deteriorated until she was unable to walk. Through a friend, a medical student, she entered a good hospital, and had a successful operation. Liberation came during recuperation there.

The names of the streets were confusing after liberation, since the Germans had renamed many of the streets in Amsterdam, especially those that had previously been named for Jewish politicians and artists. Ironically, the street in the German town of Hillersleben, where my family lived between liberation and repatriation, was named Adolf Hitlerstrasse. When I wrote to my parents from Holland, I was forced to use that obnoxious address.

———■   ■———

Sunday evening, June 20, 1945

My dearest little lady,

This coming Tuesday someone is going to Amsterdam, and I want to make use of the opportunity! We are hopeful that, in all likelihood, the quarantine will be lifted this Tuesday. For the moment, we are more or less locked in; but on the other hand, these few days give us a good opportunity to rest, something we, of course, need badly. Furthermore, I can read; there are books and periodicals at our disposal; I play chess, and the food is quite decent, so I can manage well for these few days. Before I forget it, caught up in the emotions of my first written contact with you (my letter from the day before yesterday), I forgot to send my regards to Josette. I do it now with this letter! Too bad that your parents had to stay back, but I hear that the care there is quite excellent. I hope that you see them soon.

Monday afternoon

What do you say about my luck? My sister, Betty, just came to visit me! She will hand you this little letter tomorrow. She will tell you everything. She of course knows all about Manja and me and us. She is amazingly strong, and I am sure you will like her right away. We will leave here tomorrow or the day after tomorrow; so sweet darling, we will see each other very soon now. How I long for that I cannot tell you.

I had my medical examination today, and the spotted typhus left a pleurisy. A doctor in Amsterdam will have to examine me, and tell me how I should live with it. Fortunately, it is not serious. Bye, sweetheart, I hope to see you the day after tomorrow.

Many, many kisses

your Jaap

Ina:

When I saw Jaap for the first time after liberation, I couldn't believe how skinny and how bald he was! Compared to me, since I had been home a little while and looked well, he seemed especially pathetic. I remember thinking, "What am I going to do with this fellow?" But then when I realized that we were at last together—freely—with no more interferences or encumbrances, or imprisonment to separate us, it was as if some divine intervention had taken place. I remembered what he was like during those many months, and how he inspired me to keep going, how he urged me to keep believing, to be strong. I had Jaap, and we were together; and I was going to help him regain his strength, and he'd be well again. We looked at each other; we were ecstatic; we had each other; we were together–really together–finally.

———■ ■———

Jack Polak
Accountant and Tax consultant
Reggestraat/

Member of the Netherlands Institute of Tax Consultants
Member of the Dutch Assoc. of Accountants
and Office Administration
AMSTERDAM Z.
Postgiro 3251582515
Municipality transfer p 3214
Telephone 29819

Wednesday, September 7, 1945

My sweetest darling,

   We are now at the eve of our Jewish New Year. And according to old Jewish practice, we write a Rosh Hashana letter to those we love most. I don't have to tell you how I learn to love you more and more. You are now truly a part of my life. My dear sweetheart, the coming year will be the most important year that anyone can imagine. We will be married very soon, I hope, and have our love witnessed before God. Always have confidence in me, as I hope I can also always have in you. Then we will have a beautiful life together!

   May Our Good Lord, who up until now saved both of our lives, give us the greatest happiness that a couple can have in the coming year; and may He do the same for many years to come.

   Jaap

——— ■   ■ ———

Amsterdam
September 7, 1945

My dearest boy,

What a surprise this morning! The beautiful roses and fine letter. My first red roses that I have ever received in the true meaning of the words "red roses." I take it that I received them for three reasons: Rosh Hashanah, our return to our own home, and for September 7, the day that you officially spoke with Father. So darling, also threefold thanks!

Sweetheart, this year will surely bring us a lot of good things and happiness, I am sure of it. I hope never to betray your trust in me; my trust in you is as strong as a rock! If I ever do anything that displeases you, always tell me, and give me a hard time every once in a while. I don't get that often enough, and it is so good for me.

Much, much love, good things, and many more years, not only with me but also with all of your surviving loved ones.

A heartfelt Rosh Hashana kiss from your

Ina

———— ■■ ————

EPILOGUE

EPILOGUE

Ina Soep and Jaap Polak were married on Tuesday, January 29, 1946, in a neighborhood synogogue, one of the few functioning Jewish houses of worship in Amsterdam. They arrived by horse and carriage. There were no cars available, since the rubber for auto tires and gasoline were non-existent. The same post-war shortage existed with housing, so they were forced to rent rooms with "kitchen privileges" in someone's apartment. Their next move was to a full floor in a large villa where their first child, Frederick Benno, was born on November 8 of that same year. A second son, Anthony Gerald, was born on March 4, 1949. About this time Ina's father began urging the couple to consider a move to the United States. When the Korean War broke out, fear mounted that Russia would wage war on the side of North Korea, forcing the United States to come to the aid of South Korea, thereby precipitating another World War. Western Europe might then be overrun and occupied again by a hostile power.

In 1949, Jaap traveled to the United States to determine the possibility of establishing himself in business; but the country was experiencing a recession, so he returned to Holland with discouraging news. In the course of 1950, his father-in-law set up a small wholesale diamond business in New York City, where Jaap worked during the day while studying accountancy in the evening. In 1953, when *Mr. Soep died, Jaap was thrust into the position of managing all his diamond interests in Amsterdam, New York, and Chicago, which he slowly liquidated during the next ten years. In the meantime, Jaap switched his profession as an accountant to that of an investment-adviser, a profession he had already honed as a "hobby" when, after the war, many widows of his former clients returning to Holland needed advice on how to manage their finances. He realized this was his true calling, and he could use his skills as an accountant for the benefit of his new profession. He once joked that he was an accountant by profession, in the diamond business by marriage, and an investment counselor by choice.

So the Polak family had finally moved to the United States in 1951, and settled into a private home in Eastchester , NewYork,a suburb of New York City. Jaap made frequent trips toAmsterdam until the liquidation of the Soep factory was accomplished. On November 17,1955, a daughter, Margrit Betty, was born to the couple.

Fred, their eldest son, who is a partner in a law firm in New Jersey, is married to Carrie Sills, and with their children, Joshua Andrew and Ann Elyse reside in Westfield, New Jersey. Joshua graduated from Harvard Law School, cum laude, and is an

---

In 1952, on his sixtieth birthday, Abraham Soep was knighted in The Netherlands by the then Queen Juliana, for his leadership and services to the government in restoring the war-ravaged diamond industry of Amsterdam.

associate in a Manhattan law firm. Ann is a graduate of Skidmore College and is in the Master's Program at Teacher's College, Columbia University.

Tony and his wife, Amy Moss, live in Greenwich, Connecticut with their children, Jamie Moss and Emily Lauren. Jamie is a graduate of George Washington University ,and works in research at a brokerage firm. Emily graduated magna cum laude from the University of Pennsylvania and will continue her studies leading to a PhD in Psychology. Tony has chosen his father's profession, and has his own firm in New York.

Their daughter, Margrit is a professional talent manager, and lives in Los Angeles, California, with her husband, Harvey Shield, a musician, and their daughter , Sofia Bettina. Sofia is a fifth grader in a Hebrew day school.

Manja, Jaap's first wife, currently lives near Arnhem in a nursing home. Ina and Jaap have remained friends with her all through their married years, and visit with her when they travel to Holland. She in turn, has always been interested in the Polak children. She never remarried.

Ina and Jaap have been married fifty-five years. On his 80th birthday, December 31, 1992, Queen Beatrix of The Netherlands presented him with a knighthood with the rank of Officer in the Order of Orange Nassau. This honor was bestowed upon Jaap in recognition of his many endeavors in making the American people, especially children, aware of the experiences of the Dutch people during World War II, their suffering during the German occupation, and his own experiences in the Holocaust.

There is particular significance attached to this honor since Jaap received this as an American, as a Jew, a Holocaust survivor, and as a former Dutchman living in the United States.

Since the founding of the Anne Frank Center, U.S.A., Jaap has been a Director, then President, and now Chairman Emeritus of the organization located in New York City. The Center has given him the ideal forum from which to disseminate information about the Holocaust, and create an awareness of the experiences of survivors, particularly the Dutch Jews. He is an indefatigable publicist for extolling the horrors of the Holocaust, and keeping the memory of its inhumanity alive. Jaap has become an authority on the Dutch-Jewish experience, and a consultant on Jewish affairs for the Dutch Consulate. He is still a Certified Dutch tax consultant, and, as such, he still assists other survivors in making claims for compensation. And in his role as lay historian, he is in constant demand as a speaker everywhere in the United States, to relate his experiences to audiences in schools, universities, and religious groups of all denominations.

Together, Ina and Jaap Polak have infused their lives and their childrens' education with Dutch culture. In their home, one can find many examples typical of Dutch family life: five state Bibles, many Dutch paintings, a substantial collection in their library about the resistance in Holland during World War II, Dutch tiles and silver, and family heirlooms. They have attempted to create, in their words, "an American life with a Dutch atmosphere."

DOCUMENTS

```
Name: ___Soep_____

Vorname: _Catharina_____

geboren: _____3.1.23____ Bar: _3_✓_

Laut Entscheidung Lagerkommandantur
ist Ihre          Sperrung aufgehoben.
Lager Westerbork, den 5.2.__1944
                    Dienstbereich 2
                    Verwaltung


Familienangehoerige:
```

This document of February 5, 1944, decreed that the
"promise" of being sent to Bergen-Belsen was canceled,
which placed Ina in the very dangerous position of being
sent to Auschwitz since she was hospitalized at the time,
and almost all hospital patients were evacuated for
deportation.

A Red Cross-Jewish Agency statement dated January
25, 1944, stating that Jacob Polak and his family have
been registered on the 6th Veteran Zionist List for
immigration into Palestine on an exchange for Germans
then in Palestine. On the basis of this document, Jaap and
his wife were sent to Bergen-Belsen. (see opposite page)

COMITÉ INTERNATIONAL DE LA CROIX-ROUGE
GENÈVE (Suisse)   Im Po H
                                   FD. gm

DEMANDEUR — ANFRAGESTELLER — ENQUIRER

Nom - Name .... JEWISH AGENCY

Prénom - Vorname - Christian name ....

Rue - Strasse - Street ....

Localité - Ortschaft - Locality .... JERUSALEM

Département - Provinz - County ....

Pays - Land - Country .... Palestine

Message à transmettre — Mitteilung — Message
(25 mots au maximum, nouvelles de caractère strictement personnel et
familial) — (nicht über 25 Worte, nur persönliche Familiennachrichten) —
(not over 25 words, family news of strictly personal character).

Message of 10th.1.44: "please inform Jaco POLAK -
FREIBLENDY and family, Netherlands Red Cross, AMS-
TERDAM, that they have been registered on 6th veteran zionist list for immigration into palestine
& 1 exchange. Their number is M/438/43/f/309; foreign office will communicate name to protecting
                                        power."

Date - Datum   25.1.1944

DESTINATAIRE — EMPFANGER — ADDRESSEE

Nom - Name .... JOODSCHE RAAD

Prénom - Vorname - Christian name ....

Rue - Strasse - Street .... Jan van Eijckstr. 15

Localité - Ortschaft - Locality .... AMSTERDAM

Province - Provinz - County ....

Pays - Land - Country .... Hollande

REPONSE AU VERSO   ANTWORT UMSEITIG   REPLY OVERLEAF
Prié d'écrire très lisiblement · Bitte sehr deutlich schreiben · Please write very clearly

213

A "special pass" issued to Jaap Polak permitting him to use the streetcar in Amsterdam. It could only be used from 7:00 A.M. to 7:30 P.M.; and it was invalid from Saturday at 3:00 P.M. until Monday at 6:00 A.M. The red "J" indicates it was given to a Jew. Only 100 of these passes were distributed in 1942-43, and although it was not officially stated, he was not allowed to sit down.

This is a statement of citizenship issued by the Consul-General of the Republic of El Salvador which claims that the Soep family are citizens of that country and should be protected as such. In all probability, this document saved Ina's family from being sent from Bergen-Belsen to an extermination camp in February 1945.

CONSULADO GENERAL
DE LA REPUBLICA DE EL SALVADOR, C.A.
GINEBRA
SUIZA

DosS.523/944.

BESTAETIGUNG ÜBER STAATSANGEHÖRIGKEIT.
==

Das Generalkonsulat der Republik von ·El· ·Salvador in
Genf bestätigt hiermit..............................,....

SOEP ABRAHAM geb.am I7.IV.I892,

SOEP TONI FREDERICA geb.KAUFMANN,geboren am 8.XII.I895.

SOEP CATHARINA geb.am 3.I.I923.

SOEP JOSETT geb.am I3.VIII÷I924.

dass sie als Staatsbürger von El Salvador mit all den damit ver-
bundenen Rechten und Pflichten anerkannnt sind.

Es wird ihnen anheimgestellt,sich bei den zuständigen Be-
hörden ihren derzeitigen Aufenthaltsortes über die Möglichkeiten
einer Auswanderung zu erkundigen und dem unterfertigten Generalkonsulat Bericht zu erstatten.

Gegebenenfalls sind Passbilder neueren Datums einzusenden.
Diese Passbilder haben auf der Rückseite die legalisatorische
Bestätigung der zuständigen Behörde oder eines Notars aufzuweisen.

Ginebra,6.Februar I944.

DER SEKRETAER DES GENERALKONSULATES.

BERGEN-BELSEN CAMP AND MAP PLAN

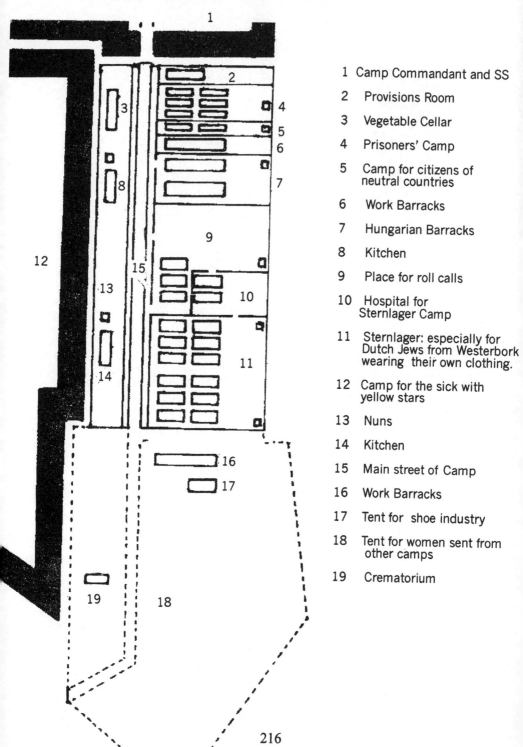

1 Camp Commandant and SS

2 Provisions Room

3 Vegetable Cellar

4 Prisoners' Camp

5 Camp for citizens of neutral countries

6 Work Barracks

7 Hungarian Barracks

8 Kitchen

9 Place for roll calls

10 Hospital for Sternlager Camp

11 Sternlager: especially for Dutch Jews from Westerbork wearing their own clothing.

12 Camp for the sick with yellow stars

13 Nuns

14 Kitchen

15 Main street of Camp

16 Work Barracks

17 Tent for shoe industry

18 Tent for women sent from other camps

19 Crematorium

As a child, I knew something was up! My parents were European immigrants, more affluent than most of our neighbors. I somehow felt different. I felt more at home in temple and Hebrew School than I did in elementary school, although my aptitude in regular school was very good. Especially in literature, reading, and drama. In Hebrew School, I had a tough time with History. I just didn't like it. Why was this? I had an early awareness that the Holocaust existed, but I think it took awhile before I associated it with my parents. I knew the Yahrzeit candle was lit on specific days of the year, and that it meant a relative had died on that day. But my grandfather had died in 1951, and what was the difference between that and my mother's brother who died at a young age? Who were my father's parents, his mother, who I was named after (Grietje)? What did their Yahrzeit lights mean? Many of my friends were without grandparents, and I guess I just knew that some people die younger than others. There was a suicide in my school, one boy died of a brain tumor,–what did my relatives die of? And why were so many of our family rituals different from not only our neighbors, but many of my Jewish friends as well. There seemed to be a "Dutch Elite" that passed through our home. Friends and relatives, beautifully dressed, always adorned with lovely jewelry, bringing young Margrit the finest of presents; dolls and glass animals from Europe, flowered pyjamas and matching robes from Saks Fifth Avenue, or the Bonnetrie in Amsterdam. Why did I eat chocolate sprinkles on bread for breakfast, and sometimes for lunch too. (In the third grade, a young black boy told me they looked like ants. I came home crying and refused to take chocolate sprinkles to school from then on.) Why were my clothes neater than other girls? Why did I wear anklets longer than they did? Why did we have exotic cheeses in our refrigerator? Why couldn't I understand what my parents said to each other half the time, and on the phone as well? Whenever they didn't want me to understand what they were saying, they spoke Dutch. Like a good little girl, I never learned the language. They also had beautiful accents; but what did that mean?

I'd seen pictures of my mother with my two, then tiny, big brothers on a boat, on which she said they'd come to America from Holland. Holland! I had such romantic, warm feelings about that country, where all these refined ladies and gentlemen came from. They even drank different drinks at cocktail hour; and there were always special crackers and nuts, cheese-flavored and cream-filled, served in pretty, fragile bowls. It all looked so wonderful. The world of religion had great importance too. My father loved temple, and I was so proud to carry his blue velvet bag with his tallis in it. The prayers and melodies were beautiful; and my father showed me books that my very own great grandfather had handwritten, for he was a scribe. This ancestor of mine painted a scroll on parchment which still hangs in our home today. It is colorful, and has beautiful designs made out of tiny Hebrew letters.

But, somewhere, there was a mixed message. The world of classical music, my grandmother's miniature silver collection which was kept under lock and key in a glass case–: with the windmills that moved, and the spinning wheel, ships, and delicate furniture; the ballet to which we brought binoculars to see the dancers close up: It seemed a front for something else. My mother was clearly uncomfortable with outdoors playing. I had a constant fear that something was going to happen to me. My father worked so hard, creating a good life for us; his feverish gulps of satisfaction. He clearly loves life, but why with more energy than someone else? Is he making up for lost time somewhere? My mother's obsession with fine things; why did I have to wear pure wool underwear that itched so terribly? I was made to feel that I must appreciate these fine fabrics, or I was crazy. Was there a time when you had no wool, Mommy? And Mommy, why do you tire so easily–3 hour naps each afternoon? And your devotion to your routine; God forbid it should sway even one bit from your intentions. What will happen to you if you don't have everything perfectly in place? Little Margrit created her own rituals for what must, and must not be. My routines included turning light switches off and on extra times, running up and down stairs, a desperate fear of saying dirty words and slang that might not please God. Even at age six, I wouldn't go into the store called Lord & Taylor, for it broke the 1st commandment. And why did I so feel the need not only to please them, but to take care of them? Why did I feel that they had wounds that needed healing? I, just a small child, who needed them to help me grow. But I felt it all the same, and I didn't understand.

I don't remember when I first discovered that my parents were Holocaust survivors. I know that my mother had pictures of two handsome young men on her desk. One was of her brother Benno, who died in the war; and the other was Rudi, who had been her boyfriend for 7 years, and was also killed. I think I could understand one young man dying, but two,–and why? Would she have married this boy if he had lived? Did she know my father at the same time? Anger, admiration, wondering if I would still be Margrit if I had been their child. Is my father jealous? My not

218

wanting my mother to love another boy; to keep a picture in her desk of him; and then–the statement that my father had had another wife!!!! Manja, the one who lives in Amsterdam and sends you gifts on your birthday. It was all too confusing. The truth had not been told.

My father and I went to sporting events together after my brothers, 7 and 9 years older than I, left for college. Soccer and tennis usually, and on the ways there and back I started asking questions. It seemed easier to approach my father, which was odd, because I shared everything about myself with my mother; and I learned from my father that my mother doesn't like to talk about the war. Well, I learned, and was still given a stilted picture of it all; for my father seemed such a hero; the suffering was so repressed that all I saw was the good,–and the horrible story of what happened to the Jews, which I, had now just begun studying in Hebrew School, was not my parents' story. · My parents fell in love in a concentration camp. What a beautiful story. He showed me their love letters, and I brought them to school for show and tell, and the story impressed everyone. I said to all my friends: "My parents met and courted in a concentration camp. One of the worst. And my father was married to a woman he didn't love, and she didn't love him, and it was all very dramatic. And they survived; and they lived happily ever after. Look at me! It's lucky they survived, because otherwise I wouldn't have been born!"

And when I decided to translate their letters, 6 years ago, I still felt that way. The idea of my mother and father truly suffering hadn't hit home. I went to survivor meetings, and children of survivor meetings, and left in disgust of those people who dwelled on their misery. Aren't they too happy they survived? But the sorrow, subconsciously, was taking its toll. My weight had dropped to 90 pounds. I had a chronic nervous skin condition, and though still considered the golden girl, the young and beautiful aspiring actress, I was grappling with the reality of grief. A grief that my parents could never express to me, and who can blame them? Except Margrit, from her childhood on up, was an extremely curious, sensitive girl; and she felt all that unexpressed pain; and she herself did not know how to express it.

Translating my mother's and father's love letters, showing the heart of their reasons to survive, has been some of the most valuable work of my life in its beginning to permit myself to feel all that locked up sadness, in my beginning to know where my heretofore seemingly irrational fears come from, and in my beginning to understand why I cannot accept many of my parent's unrealistic reactions to things easily. And in addition to this, I am creating with these letters, a valuable document of how survivors survive and move forward in their lives. I have a love story to tell, I have real people to tell it about. I have pictures, I have a vision of splendor and wealth in Amsterdam in the 30's, and diamonds and cars, and close families, and people with names, occupations, future dreams, and how these dreams were in ninety-nine percent of the cases shattered. My parents took those dreams that they wrote about in Bergen-Belsen, horror of all concentration camps, and fulfilled them. I owe this book to them, myself, and to my future husband, and our future children, to a public who does not yet understand what happened.

The face inside the front cover was unmistakable. I could recognize the fine, distinct features anywhere, although I knew them as marked by age. Yet, in 51 years, the profile had not changed. My grandmother's face stared back at me as my eyes filled with tears. For as long as I can remember I have known the story of my grandparents' past. It seems as if it was never told to me. I just always knew it.

Visiting the Holocaust Museum was an experience I believed I was prepared for. I now know that no one can ever be prepared for the visions inside the perfectly architectured walls in Washington, D.C. The list of victims' names scaling three levels, the freight car's dark, musty feel, and the smell of the shoe exhibit all add to the feelings that overwhelm a person. After leaving the museum I questioned what gave my grandparents the strength to keep fighting. Why would they want to live after all they had been through? I can only imagine that they did not want to give up. There was no way they would let the other side win. Their lives meant victory.

When entering the Holocaust Museum, everyone receives a booklet following one person through the war. After completing the final floor, I turned to the last page of my book only to find my person had died. I was devastated, and I searched for some comfort. I asked a friend if her person had survived or not. When she said yes, I grabbed her book. I opened it up expecting to find a stranger who now lived somewhere in Israel with many grandchildren. Instead, I found my grandmother. Catharina Soep had been twenty years old when she was interned in the Westerbork transit camp. At twenty-two she was liberated from Bergen-Belsen. Eight months later, she married Jack Polak and had three children. That was the story inside the book. That is the story of my family.

Having family who survived the Holocaust has always impacted upon my life. However, at no other time did it affect me as much as when I saw my grandmother, like millions of others, inside a book. I consider my grandparents to be two of the most extraordinary people I have ever met. Having the strength to fall in love under the control of Hitler and to survive, has made them stronger than I will ever be. I admire their strength and courage. They have inspired me to keep pushing myself until I achieve all my goals. I have now visited the Holocaust Museum twice. I understand that, as many times as I return, it will always affect me in a different way. Seeing my grandmother's young, innocent face defined my first visit. I will

221

never forget the sadness that came over me when I connected the woman I know to the experiences I had always known about. That sadness is important for me to remember. It reminds me that somewhere inside of me is a part of her, a part that never gives up.

Written by our grand-daughter, Emily Polak, 1997.

The New Yorker would not approve of this essay. In an October 6 article, Cynthia Ozick, an important and widely respected writer, indicates that the focus of Anne Frank's diary should be on the cruelties and injustices of society rather than on Anne's spirit and magnetic personality. Upon reading this, I became distraught. I agree that it is extremely important to learn about the atrocities of the Holocaust, but the aspect of the diary which had the greatest effect on me was Anne's dynamic character. What if a college admissions officer, having read *The New Yorker*, were to read my thoughts about Anne and conclude that I was trivializing the true significance of the young girl's diary? The reality, though, is that I, like many teenagers, feel a personal connection to Anne Frank, even though my circumstances in 1997 are in no way comparable to hers. Wrestling with my options, I finally decided that these are my thoughts and feelings, and they are worth the risk.

When my grandfather gave me The Diary of Anne Frank, I remember being somewhat mystified that I had just been handed a copy of the second most-read book in the world (the Bible being the first). However, I soon realized why he had given me this book. It was because my grandmother and grandfather experienced the same discrimination as Anne, each being sent to the Bergen-Belsen concentration camp. More importantly, however, it was because my grandfather believed in this girl and her message so deeply that he eventually became the President of the Anne Frank Center USA. I therefore approached the diary with great expectations. I wanted to decide for myself if this girl deserved the respect and admiration she received, not only from my grandfather but also from the world.

"I want to live on, even after death." In April of 1944, Anne Frank made this bold yet innocent statement having not the slightest idea of the degree to which she would "live on," affecting the entire world with her writing. Anne Frank wrote from a naive yet profound viewpoint that endears her to anyone who encounters her journal. I related to her immediately. At age 13, I understood the growing-up issues with which she was dealing. We were both adjusting to adolescence. We were learning to deal with boys, our families, as well as changes in our bodies. Re-reading the diary at age 17, I have gained new insight and have a deeper understanding of Anne Frank and the workings of her mind. She thought

223

about society and her role within it. Even at her young age, she realized that she was not the focus of the world but rather was able to focus on the world. At 13, I connected with the adolescence in Anne Frank; at 17, I connect with the maturity of her mind.

Through her journal, I found we share an uncommon energy, a love of life, an ever-growing curiosity, a desire to understand, a gift of apt expression, and a lively spirit. We are both strong people with a will to persevere. Her journal provided her an outlet for the abundance of thoughts she had exploding within her. In it, she was thoughtful and expressive, yet sometimes headstrong and opinionated as well. Like her, I have a lot to say and, like her, I have written in a journal throughout my life. An extremely vocal person, I hold strong beliefs and am not afraid to voice my opinions. Whether in a classroom, in my synagogue, in my clubs, or in a friend's basement, I assert my views on such controversial subjects as genetic testing, female rabbis, or rap music.

Despite her desperate situation, Anne Frank had an exuberance about her, an extreme love for life. Always wanting to know more and understand why, she questioned everything around her, even in her isolated life in the annex. I too am a vivacious, inquisitive person, with a passion for life and its mysteries. I bring to each of my endeavors excitement and enthusiasm, be it on the tennis court or in a court of law. I slam the fuzzy yellow sphere with all of my concentration and intensity; I entrap the witness during a mock trial competition, my questions precise and pointed. My energy cannot be contained, nor can my curiosity. Inside a classroom or outside on a mountainside, I can never know enough or push myself too far. A formula is meaningless without understanding, just as life is meaningless without exploration and discovery. I want to experience everything and conquer every challenge life has to offer. Only then will I be true to myself and to Anne Frank, who never had the chance.

As The Diary of Anne Frank will continue to sit prominently in my bookcase, the impact of Anne Frank will continue to live inside me. She is a constant reminder to cherish my liberty and never to give up hope. I am not so bold as to say that I want to live on after death, but I will say that I want to live my life passionately and to its fullest. I am fortunate to have been both emotionally and intellectually touched by Anne Frank. Now it is my turn to touch the world.

Speech given by our son, Frederick Polak,
on Holocaust Remembrance Day, early 90's.

It was a miracle that I am able to stand before you today. I was born in The Netherlands in 1946, less than two years after my parents returned from the concentration camp at Bergen-Belsen. Before the war there were 140,000 Jews in Holland; less than 25,000 survived. As the allied forces moved east, the Germans evacuated Bergen-Belsen with the intent of eliminating all the survivors. They put my father on a train and attempted to starve everyone on the train. When my father was liberated by the Russians, he had typhus. Ninety-five percent of those with typhus died; my father survived, weighing 80 pounds. My mother was put on another train. It carried 2,400 persons and the orders were to drive the train into the Elbe River. Fortunately, the allied forces came first. My father's parents perished in Sobibor. My mother's brother in Mauthausen; one of my father's sisters died from typhus three days after liberation. So you see, it is a miracle that I am here.

About eight years ago, my father wrote about the High Holidays in September, 1945 in Amsterdam, the first time since the early 1940's that he was able to celebrate the High Holidays in a Synagogue. He wrote as follows:

"It was a service of thanksgiving and tears. We were reminded of those who died, and in every row we visualized the wonderful men and women who were not there anymore. Many times during the services and in all the years thereafter, and even today I ask myself, "Why me?—and although more than 33 years have passed, on each holiday the long, long list of relatives, friends, and acquaintances goes through my mind; and all I can say to myself, but also to all of you, is 'The fact that you survived and belonged to this small percentage puts extra responsibility on your shoulders to do the work that these millions of people otherwise would have done.'"

Each of us has been touched by the Holocaust, whether it was the death of a close relative, or the loss of a long-lost relative. So, too, should each of us ask ourselves, as my father has, "Why me?" And in answering that question for ourselves, each of us should recognize our obligation to our people: to carry forward the faith and the tradition of those who have not been so fortunate as we, the survivors of a people Hitler attempted to

225

eliminate from the face of the earth.

Carrie, Ann, and I recently celebrated Josh's Bar Mitzvah. It was about the happiest day of my life. As my father said his aliyah, he was overcome with emotion at what was occurring. At that moment so was I, his son. I had certain thoughts then which had coalesced somewhat since then, and I want to close by expressing them to you tonight. Josh is the first grandchild of Holocaust survivors to be Bar Mitzvahed. He carries forward our name into Jewish manhood. But he carries more than that:–the memory of his great-grandparents, his great-uncle, and his great-aunt who perished, of the six million who perished. And he carries forward a pledge to teach his children and grandchildren to never forget what happened, and that they learn from what happened. And I ask each of you today to do the same for your children and grandchildren.